JCJC#
JSTO

D1171645

A FORGE OF
FREEDOM BOOK

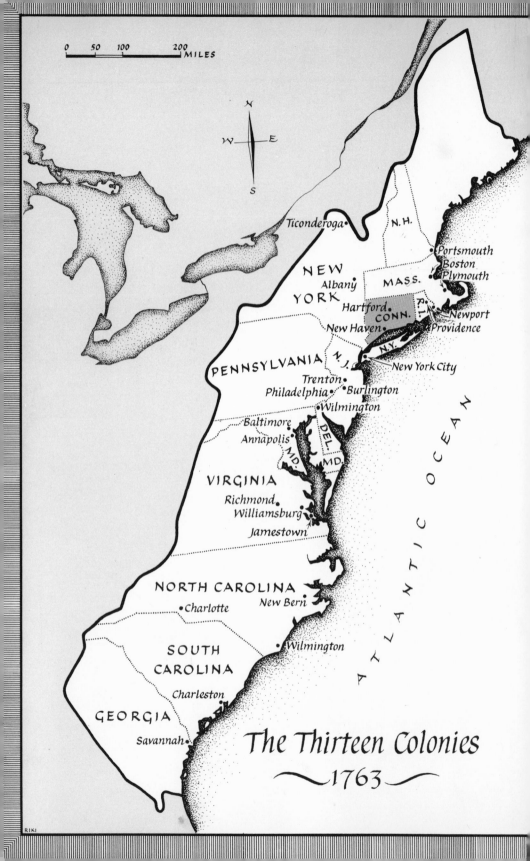

The Thirteen Colonies
—1763—

0 50 100 200 MILES

N
W E
S

Ticonderoga

N. H.

NEW YORK

Albany

MASS.

Portsmouth
Boston
Plymouth

Hartford
New Haven

CONN.

R.I.

Newport
Providence

N.Y.

PENNSYLVANIA

N. J.

New York City

Trenton
Philadelphia   Burlington
Wilmington

Baltimore
Annapolis

DEL.

MD.

MD.

VIRGINIA

Richmond
Williamsburg
Jamestown

NORTH CAROLINA

Charlotte   New Bern

SOUTH CAROLINA

Wilmington

Charleston

GEORGIA

Savannah

ATLANTIC OCEAN

RIKI

THE
CONNECTICUT
COLONY

by

Johanna Johnston

CROWELL-COLLIER PRESS
Collier-Macmillan Limited, London

Library of Congress Catalog Card Number: 69-19576

The Macmillan Company
Collier-Macmillan Canada Ltd., Toronto, Ontario
Printed in the United States of America

FIRST PRINTING

PICTURE CREDITS

The Bettmann Archive, Inc., 18, 40; Culver Pictures, Inc.,
19, 27, 30, 39, 52–53, 59, 64, 68, 71, 84, 90, 93, 97, 99, 102,
107, 113, 118, 121; Historical Pictures Service—Chicago, 2,
8–9, 12, 14, 16, 22, 34, 43, 46, 49, 66, 73, 79, 104, 123; Virginia
State Library, 74.

JACKET ILLUSTRATION: *The hiding of the Charter in the Oak*

For Annabelle and
all the Dirks
who introduced me to
Connecticut

CONTENTS

I. Explorations
and Invitations

The Connecticut Colony has a very special distinction among the original thirteen. Its settlers were the first colonists to work out a truly democratic form of government for themselves. They drew up for their guidance what historians have called the world's first written constitution. Those achievements stand out like early markers on the trail that one day led to a union of the thirteen colonies under a government "based on the consent of those governed."

But there were unique events in Connecticut's history even before those historic accomplishments. What other colony, for instance, can record that white men were urged to settle in the region by Indians—Indians so eager to have white neighbors that they offered yearly supplies of corn and furs to any Englishmen who would move in near them?

This unusual invitation was made in 1631. Waginacut, a sachem, or chief, of a small Connecticut tribe, took two

Governor Edward Winslow of the Plymouth Colony.

of his braves with him and traveled north and east to the English colonies in the Massachusetts territory. They visited Governor John Winthrop of the Massachusetts Bay Colony and then Governor Edward Winslow of the Plymouth Colony.

One of Waginacut's braves, who was named Jack Straw, could speak a little English. He served as an interpreter for Waginacut when the sachem described the land from which the Indians came. They lived on the banks of a great river, he told the English governors—the Quinnequktuqut, or Long River. Its waters were full of fish. Along its banks were rich meadows where corn grew in the summer and deer browsed in the fall and spring. There were also forests where much fine game could be caught, both for food and fur. Speaking through Jack Straw, Waginacut promised the English governors that if they would send settlers to that pleasant territory his tribe would provide them with eighty beaver skins a year along with much corn.

Waginacut did not hide his reason for making such a cordial invitation. He and his people wanted English help and protection against strong enemy tribes that lived on either side of them. To the west of the region where they lived were the great Mohawk hunting grounds along the Hudson River. The Mohawks, as Waginacut tried to make clear, were among the most ferocious of all Indians. "Hadree, hadree, succomee, succomee," they cried as they ran into battle—"We come, we come, to suck your blood." So fierce were the Mohawks that they had driven away another strong tribe, the Pequots, from their original camping grounds farther south along the Hudson.

But the Pequots had fled the Mohawk country only to take refuge in the lands to the east of the Long River. Now, with the Pequots to the east of them and the Mohawks to the west, the River Indians lived in a state of terror and subjection. Both Pequots and Mohawks made regular visits to the villages along the river, demanding tribute from the River Indians if they wanted to save their crops, their wigwams, their very lives. A Pequot band had only recently attacked a tribe of River Indians who lived very close to Waginacut's village. The sachem of that tribe had been driven into exile. After that Waginacut had decided to visit the Englishmen and ask for help.

The Mohawks and the Pequots feared very little but they did "fear the white-faced man with his hot-mouth weapon," Waginacut said.

Both governors were interested in what the sachem had to say, but neither one was able to promise a journey of inspection just at that time. Waginacut and his companions returned to their village on the Long River, their invitation unaccepted.

The Long River, or Quinnequktuqut, of which they spoke, was not unknown to white men at this time. It had been discovered, explored and claimed by the Dutch seventeen years before. In 1614 Captain Adrian Block had sailed from the tiny Dutch settlement on Manhattan Island at the mouth of the Hudson River on a voyage of exploration eastward, through Long Island Sound, which Block called the Great Bay. On that voyage he sailed along the coast of what is now Connecticut, anchored briefly at the mouth of the Housatonic River, which he named the River of the Red Hills, and then sailed on to the Connecticut (Quinnequktuqut) River. This river he entered. Finding that the ocean tides did not carry far inland, he called it the Varshe, or Fresh, River and continued sailing up its waters.

It was springtime. The trees and vines along the river's edge were freshly green. So were the meadows that interrupted the forests now and then—meadows which the Indians kept clear by burning them over every fall. Every so often Block passed an Indian village or encampment. When he had sailed up the river to the point where the city of Hartford now stands, he saw a fortified village, surrounded by palisades. (This was the village which would be attacked by the Pequots some years later, thus inspiring Waginacut to ask help from the English. Its Indian name was Suckiaug.) Block anchored here and went ashore.

The Indians were planting corn. A great oak tree on a knoll a little distance from the river was just beginning to come into leaf. Later, settlers in that area would learn that it was the Indian custom to plant corn when the leaves on that oak were the size of a mouse's ear. The Indians often held council meetings under the great oak, and they had many legends about the majestic tree.

Block found the Indians at Suckiaug friendly. When he made it known that he wanted to trade for furs, they brought him many pelts of beaver, fox and bear. They were delighted with the trinkets he gave them in exchange.

For two weeks Block lingered with the Indians at Suckiaug. Then he continued his voyage up the river. At Enfield Falls the river became impassable, so he turned about and headed back down the river and out into the Sound.

Continuing his exploration, he sailed farther east along the Connecticut coast, passing the mouth of the Thames River and then following the coast of what is now Rhode Island. Changing course a little, he discovered the island which today is called Block Island after him. Then he went on exploring the New England coast as far as Boston harbor.

When Block finally returned to the Dutch trading post on Manhattan with a rich cargo of furs, he was full of enthusiasm for the country he had found. He drew a map of his explorations, showing the coast of Connecticut, the Connecticut River as far as the Falls, and the coast of Rhode Island as well.

Captain Block's expedition, and his map of the territory he had traveled, gave the Dutch all they needed to claim this area as theirs. And they began at once to make the most of the region in the way that seemed most important to them—fur trading.

Dutch sloops and schooners began to sail along the Connecticut coast and up the Connecticut River, trading with all the Indian tribes along the waterways. The Dutch traders got along well with the Indians. Their fur trade brought greater and greater profits to them and to the men in Holland who were backing them. But somehow the Dutch never thought of establishing settlements in the Connecticut area as they had on Manhattan Island, and as the English had in Massachusetts and Virginia. Connecticut was simply fur country to them.

This lack of Dutch interest in settling Connecticut was probably what prompted Waginacut to appeal to the English colonists some years later, when he wanted the protection of white men as neighbors. This same lack of interest in settlement would finally cause the Dutch to lose the Connecticut territory to the English in spite of their claims to it by discovery and exploration. For the English *were* settlers and town builders. They had keen eyes for good farming land. "It is a sin to let such rich land, which produces such fine corn, lie uncultivated," an English governor told a Dutch navigator after he had visited Connecticut. Above all, the English were settlers because most of them had emigrated to America for religious reasons and were seeking new homes before anything else.

The English began investigating the Connecticut territory a year after Waginacut's visit to Massachusetts. Edward Winslow, governor of the Plymouth Colony, had not forgotten the sachem's description of the country. In the summer of 1632, he made an expedition to the Connecticut River valley. Most historians consider him the first Englishman to visit Connecticut. Winslow was so pleased with what he saw that, before he returned to Plymouth, he bought land from one of the River Indian sachems a few miles upriver from the village of Suckiaug.

The Dutch soon heard about Governor Winslow's visit and his purchase of land and it occurred to them that perhaps it was time they established some signs of their ownership. Their little settlement on Manhattan Island was now called New Amsterdam. Wouter Van Twiller was the town's governor. Van Twiller decided that a few forts along the Connecticut River might be a good idea. He arranged for the purchase from the Indians of a point of land at the mouth of the Connecticut River. The Dutch coat of arms was nailed to a tree. The point was named Kievit's Hook and there was talk of building a fort there which would control the entrance to the river.

The next year Van Twiller sent out another party under the leadership of Jacob Van Curler with instructions to see that a fort was actually built somewhere up the river. Van Curler sailed up the river into the neighborhood of Suckiaug. However, instead of parleying with the River Indians about buying land, Van Curler and his men bargained with the Pequots who had harassed the River Indians for so long and who claimed that all the River Indian property was Pequot land. The Dutch finally bought a piece of land one mile long and one third of a mile wide from the Pequot sachem and paid him twenty-eight yards of cloth for it, plus six axes, six kettles, eighteen knives, one sword blade, one pair of shears and some toys.

On this piece of land Van Curler and his men built a small fort. They armed it with two small cannon and named it the House of Hope. And although they had traded with the Pequots for the land, their aim was to be friendly with all the Indians in the area. They told both the River Indians and the Pequots that the area around the fort was to be peaceful territory from now on. No attacks between hostile Indians were to be made on Dutch ground. At last the Dutch were beginning to claim the territory they had discovered. Unfortunately they were a little late.

Governor Winslow had returned to Plymouth after his visit to the Connecticut valley full of praise for the richness of the country. As a result, several small vessels from Plymouth beat their way some distance up the Connecticut River in the summer of 1633, stopping here and there to trade for furs with the Indians. Several boats from the Massachusetts Bay Colony also made the trip. In July Governor Winslow suggested to Governor Winthrop that the Plymouth and Massachusetts Bay colonies establish a joint trading post somewhere on the Connecticut River. The Massachusetts Bay governor was doubtful about the project and so Winslow decided that the Plymouth Colony should make the attempt alone. He commissioned one of the Plymouth colonists, William Holmes, to carry out the scheme. In September of 1633, Holmes and a few men set out in a small ship. With them, they took an already constructed frame of a building designed as a trading post.

Their destination was that part of the river above Sucki-aug where Winslow had purchased land from the River Indians. The voyage there would take them past the new Dutch fort, the House of Hope.

As they sailed slowly into view of the fort, they heard a sudden roll of drums from within it and then saw men running to the two cannon outside. The little ship from Plymouth came almost abreast of the fort. Van Curler, the fort's commander, shouted at the English captain to strike his ship's sails.

Holmes called back that he had a commission from the governor of Plymouth to go up the river and that he intended to do so.

For several minutes no one could guess what would happen next. The Dutch stood at their cannon, looking to Van Curler for an order to fire. The little English ship continued on her way. Van Curler gave no order. And so the English ship quietly passed the fort and moved on up the river.

Site of the Dutch Fort of Good Hope.

Holmes anchored a few miles above the village of Suckiaug, and traded with the River Indian sachem for more land near the acreage that Governor Winslow had bought the year before. The River Indians were naturally pleased to have the English trading with them for land which they considered theirs by right of heredity. The Pequots, on the other hand, who considered themselves lords of the region by right of conquest, were not pleased. The first seeds of conflict between the Pequots and the English were sown, though they would not burst into the open for some time.

The frame for the trading house was unloaded, set up, and the house was finished off. And the trouble, it seemed, was coming from the Dutch. Angered by the bold English move of establishing a trading post in what the Dutch considered their territory, Governor Van Twiller sent a force of seventy men from New Amsterdam to order Holmes and the English out of the area.

But Holmes and his men were determined to hold their new post. When the Dutch force approached, the defenders manned their guns and appeared so ready to resist to the last man that the Dutch troops hesitated. Finally, in the same sort of way that Van Curler had let the English ship pass his fort without action, the Dutch troops turned around and went back to the House of Hope.

William Holmes's success in establishing an English trading post in Connecticut in 1633 seemed like a signal for a rush of English settlers to the area. During the next few years, three towns—Windsor, Hartford and Wethersfield —were founded along the Connecticut River within a ten-mile range of the fort. Still another English outpost, Saybrook, was established forty miles south at the mouth of the river. And just a few years later the town of New Haven was founded on the Connecticut coast at the mouth of the Quinnipiac River.

Although the trading post had been established by the Plymouth Colony, the chief settlers in the area upriver near it were emigrants from the Massachusetts Bay Colony. The Three River Towns established by these emigrants became the original Connecticut Colony. This colony would be the first testing ground of democracy in America.

II. The First Settlements

The guiding genius of the Connecticut Colony, the man who inspired its great experiment, was Thomas Hooker, a Puritan minister.

Hooker had suffered for his religious beliefs in the same way that many Puritans suffered in England during the reigns of King James and his son, Charles I. He had been the pastor of a Puritan church in London, much loved and admired by his congregation. But authorities of the Church of England, the only church that was supposed to exist in England, according to Charles I, had forced Hooker's church to close. The members of the church were then so watched and spied upon that many of them sailed overseas to settle in the Massachusetts Bay Colony. Hooker, no longer able to preach, had turned to teaching school. But the church authorities still pursued him and he was summoned to appear before a royal commission to be judged for his nonconforming beliefs. Instead, Hooker fled to Holland. Letters from former members of his congregation who

Thomas Hooker— from the design for the Hooker Memorial Window in Center Church, Hartford, Connecticut.

had settled in America came to him, urging him to join them. Finally, in 1633, Hooker decided to do so. Along with some two hundred Puritans who had gathered around him in Holland, he sailed for America.

Somehow though, the hardships that Thomas Hooker suffered for his faith did not make him intolerant of those who believed differently from him. He had a generous attitude toward the world and his fellow man, an attitude that was shared by very few of the Puritans of the Massachusetts Bay Colony, particularly the leaders. Most Massachusetts Bay people, and Plymouth people, too, believed that they had traveled thousands of miles and faced innumerable hardships to create a perfect church community. In their view, anyone who was not a part of the church was not part of the community and hardly even welcome. Anyone who disagreed with the leaders of the church either over church doctrine or town policy was liable to be expelled from the community.

The differences between Thomas Hooker and the leading Puritans of the Bay Colony did not show up all at once. Hooker and his companions were welcomed by Governor Winthrop. They were assigned land in Newtown, where those members of Hooker's congregation who had come to America earlier had settled. It was one of the newest of the little towns that had grown up around the first settlement of Boston.

There was rejoicing, of course, as Hooker and his group met again with their friends. And the newcomers went to work to clear land, erect shelters and build a meetinghouse where Hooker could preach to them all.

But before long Hooker began to see signs of dissatisfaction among the settlers. In the nearby villages of Dorchester and Watertown there were various colonists who were displeased at having no voice in how they were governed because they were not church members. Hooker heard their complaints. He also heard a good deal of talk about the case of Anne Hutchinson, a brilliant and appealing woman who was holding meetings in her home for Bible study. The church leaders were threatening to expel her for discussing points of doctrine which they insisted were matters for church decision, not hers.

Hooker's position as a preacher meant that he met frequently with Governor Winthrop and other colony leaders. He spoke to them of the restlessness he sensed among some of the colonists, and he asked why all the colonists could not be given more freedom to speak about matters that affected them all.

Governor Winthrop had his own defense for the Massa-

*John Winthrop,
Governor of the Massachusetts
Bay Colony.*

chusetts policy. "The best part is always the least, and of that best part, the wiser part is always the lesser."

Hooker pondered Winthrop's words. One day, some time later, he wrote Winthrop his view: "In matters of greater consequences, which concern the common good, a general council chosen by *all*, I conceive, under favor, most suitable to rule and most safe for relief of all."

Meanwhile various men who were weary of protesting to no avail began thinking of the Connecticut country to the south and west of Massachusetts. In that wilderness, they could build their own towns and run them as they chose. Requests for permission to move were made to the church council—and denied.

In spite of that, John Oldham of Watertown set off in 1634 to investigate the Connecticut valley. He returned to Watertown with such a favorable report that he was soon leading a group of Watertown people to Connecticut where they made the beginnings of the town of Wethersfield. During the summer of the next year, 1635, several more groups left Watertown for Wethersfield. That same summer, a party of men and women from Dorchester traveled south and west to settle on land near the trading post that William Holmes of Plymouth had set up two years before. They founded the town of Windsor.

Thomas Hooker and his congregation in Newtown watched these pioneers depart and became more and more sure that the answer to their dissatisfaction in Massachusetts lay in the same direction. Another request was made to the church council for permission to move and was finally granted.

Then came disturbing news from England. Everyone planning to leave the Bay Colony for Connecticut knew that the Dutch claimed the territory. It was possible that the Dutch might dispute the right of the English to settle there, but everyone was willing to risk that chance. No one dreamed, until the summer of 1635, that there might be a conflicting English claim on the territory.

John Winthrop, Jr., son of the man who had been the Massachusetts governor for the previous two years, brought the news. Arriving in Boston after finishing his education in England, he announced that the Connecticut country, or all the land west of the Narragansett River to the South Sea (the Pacific Ocean) had been given by a royal grant to the Earl of Warwick some years before. This English grant was based on the fact that John Cabot had sailed past the Connecticut coast long before Adrian Block had mapped it, and so Cabot had claimed it for England. The grant to the Earl of Warwick had recently been acquired by a group of British noblemen who were of the Puritan faith. Since King Charles's harshness to Puritans in England was only increasing, these noblemen planned a colony in the Connecticut territory which would be a refuge for other titled and wealthy Puritans like themselves.

Two leaders of the project were Lord Say and Sele and Baron Brook. These two men had commissioned young Winthrop to set up a fort at the mouth of the Connecticut River and lay out a town there. They had appointed him "Governor of the River Connecticut" for one year.

Lord Say and Sele, one of the leaders of the project to build a colony in the Connecticut territory as a refuge for wealthy, titled Puritans.

When the Newtown people heard all this, they were troubled. They had been willing to risk a dispute with the Dutch, but they were not sure about their chances if they settled on land claimed by noblemen of their own country. A group of them hurried to talk to young John Winthrop. Before long an agreement was worked out. If they settled on land that was claimed later by Lord Say and Sele and Baron Brook they would move from it, provided there was proper recompense for the time, effort and money they had invested.

With this worry settled, a small group of Newtown people prepared to leave for Connecticut at once. Thomas Hooker and the rest of his congregation planned to follow the next spring. Hooker said a farewell prayer for the advance group. The pioneers set off. Two weeks later they arrived at the Indian village of Suckiaug. There they halted, to make the beginnings of the town that would become Hartford.

Meanwhile young John Winthrop had word that the Dutch were again becoming irritated by English invaders in their territory. He rushed off a small party of men to seize the land at the mouth of the Connecticut River and build a fort.

The English arrived just in time. They tore down the Dutch coat of arms from the tree on the point that the Dutch had named Kievit's Hook. They carved a grinning face in the bark of the tree instead. But they had barely thrown up some earthworks and set up two cannon when a Dutch ship came into view. The Dutch called out challenges. The Englishmen answered. And then, once again, as twice before, the Dutch retreated before English determination. The ship turned about and returned to New Amsterdam.

By November, John Winthrop, Jr., and a small group of men arrived at the new fort, which was called Saybrook, after its two chief backers, Lord Say and Sele and Baron Brook. With them was Lieutenant Lion Gardiner, a young civil engineer who had been appointed to survey and lay out a town as well as command the fort. Gardiner's wife was with him. She was expecting her first child, who would be born the next spring. According to legend the baby boy, named David, was the first white child born in Connecticut.

Before that cheerful event, though, there was a terrible winter. Bitterly cold weather by mid-November froze the river all the way up to the tiny new settlements of Wethersfield, Windsor and Hartford. A ship laden with winter supplies for the new settlers at Hartford could not make its way up the river. Snow whirled, wind howled and the food ran so low that some of the settlers beat their way down the river to the new fort at Saybrook. But supplies were low at the fort also. Finally the refugees from Hartford managed to loosen a small ship frozen in the harbor ice and in it they made a difficult trip back to Boston. Another group from the Hartford area struggled back to Massachusetts through the snow-buried forests. A few stayed on, getting a little corn from the Indians, and otherwise living as the Indians did in a bad winter, by hunting and eating roots and acorns.

But the weather grew milder at last. The brave ones who had held on through the winter felt a surge of hope. And

Thomas Hooker and his party traveling to Connecticut.

the men and women who had returned to Massachusetts were ready one and all to try the Connecticut adventure again, setting forth with increased supplies.

Thomas Hooker and his congregation also were ready to join the migration. During the winter they had turned over their lands and homes to new arrivals from England. Now they bundled clothing and blankets, tools, pots and seeds into packs. Hooker's wife was ill. A litter was made for her of a blanket slung between two poles which were carried by two men.

On a beautiful day in June, 1636, they left Newtown—one hundred and ten men, women and children, traveling on foot, driving before them more than a hundred cattle and pigs. There is no record of which trail they followed into the Connecticut country. There is only the record that they sang psalms as they walked through the woods and now and then shouted their joy at moving at last toward a land where they could satisfy their longings for individual dignity.

It was a year of departures from the Massachusetts colonies. Soon after Hooker and his people left the Bay Colony, Anne Hutchinson was expelled because of her so-called heresy. Roger Williams, another individualist, had already been asked to leave the Plymouth Colony. He was founding a colony of his own, Rhode Island, where every kind of religious faith was given the same tolerance. For awhile, Anne Hutchinson joined Williams in Rhode Island.

Hooker and his party traveled two weeks on their march to Connecticut. Sometimes they spent the night on the outskirts of some Indian village and shared food with the natives. Sometimes they were alone in the wilderness. Then at last they arrived at the east bank of the Connecticut River. There they halted, wondering how to transport both humans and livestock across the rushing current. Waginacut, the sachem who had first invited Englishmen to the area, came to their aid. He summoned all the nearby Indians to bring canoes and rafts to carry the group across.

Ashore on the west bank, there was a joyous commotion as Hooker and all the men, women and children with him were greeted by those who had come before. There were prayers of thanksgiving and songs of praise. Beyond the

Hooker and his friends arrive in Connecticut.

worshiping crowd, the great oak on the knoll stood massive and green in the afternoon sun. The town of Hartford was now truly begun.

For many months the settlers had no time to make any plans for the governing of their town, nor was there any real need for them to do so. When the Massachusetts Colony had finally granted their request to move, it was agreed that the Three River Towns would be under Massachusetts supervision for the first year of their settlement. Roger Ludlow, a lawyer and a good friend of Hooker's, had been appointed the local governor. A very simple "General Corte" was set up to make whatever regulations seemed necessary. Most of the regulations had to do with prohibiting the sale of guns or liquor to the Indians and keeping livestock under control of some sort. Aside from that, everyone was busy, clearing land, building shelters, digging wells, making what provisions were possible for food for the coming winter.

In the midst of this purposeful activity came the difficulty that everyone had hoped to avoid—trouble with the Pequots, trouble that built swiftly into war.

III. The Pequot War

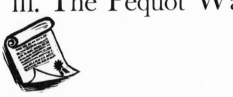

The trouble had started almost as soon as the Dutch built their trading post, the House of Hope. Defying the Dutch ruling against any Indian fighting within the area of the post, some Pequots killed several River Indians who were peacefully on their way to trade. The post commander avenged these killings by having the Pequot sachem, Woopigwooitt, killed. Such an extreme measure was bound to enrage the Pequots, but they did not retaliate at once. Their first concern was to appoint a new sachem, and this brought on difficulties within the Pequot nation. Two powerful warriors sought the honor. One was Uncas, a strong, shrewd and courageous sagamore of the Mohegan district, who was also Woopigwooitt's son-in-law. The other was Woopigwooitt's son Sassacus, almost equally renowned as a warrior. Sassacus won the loyalty of most of the Pequots and became sachem. Uncas was exiled for a while, then swore loyalty to Sassacus. But after that Uncas was so ig-

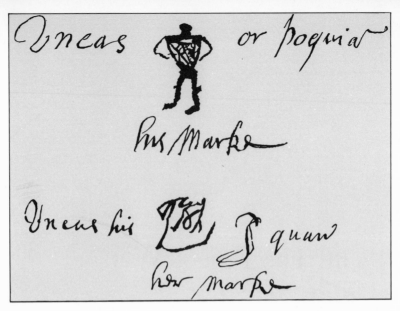

The marks, or signatures, used by Uncas and his squaw.

nored that he left the tribe with some twenty-five of his Mohegan followers and went to live near the town of Windsor. Vowing revenge on Sassacus, he waited for an opportunity to achieve it.

With Sassacus as their chief, the Pequots were ready to begin punishing the Dutch for the death of Woopigwooitt. A trader from the Virginia Colony, Captain Stone, along with eight men, was sailing up the Connecticut River in 1634. The Pequots mistook Stone for a Dutchman, climbed aboard his vessel when it was at anchor and murdered him. The Massachusetts governor sent messages to the Indians demanding that they bring Stone's murderers to English authorities for justice. No murderers were delivered.

And then, in 1636, not long after Hooker and his party arrived at Hartford, John Oldham, who had founded Wethersfield, made a trading voyage down the river to the Sound. Off Block Island a boatload of Island Indians rowed out to his pinnace and killed him and everyone else aboard.

By chance, another English vessel sailed onto the scene almost immediately afterward. The captain of that boat dealt out swift punishment to all the Indians he could find.

But when news of Oldham's death reached Boston, the Massachusetts people insisted on much more severe retaliation. They were sure also that the Pequots must have had something to do with the tragedy. Sir Henry Vane was governor of the Bay Colony in this year of 1636. He sent out a force of ninety men to punish the Block Islanders and to find out if the Pequots were harboring Oldham's killers.

The expedition only made the situation worse. The Pequots who were found swore that they had no knowledge of the Oldham murder. But the English burned their wigwams all the same, destroyed their crops and killed several braves. The Pequots were now aroused against the English as well as the Dutch.

The little fort at Saybrook was a handy target for them. All through the winter of 1636–37 Lion Gardiner and his men were subjected to hit-and-run attacks by the Pequots. Life at the fort during that winter was one long stretch of constant watchfulness interrupted by bursts of shrieking terror flashing in from the forests behind or the waters in front. But the men at the fort held on.

Spring came and the colonists at the Three Towns up the river were thankful for having endured the winter without starvation. It was time to plant crops, and hope was in the air. And then a party of Pequots descended on Wethersfield.

The settlers rallied as quickly as they could but before the Pequots were driven back, six men and three women had been killed. Twenty-one cows were killed and great damage was done to the rude homes the settlers had managed to build. As a parting gesture the Pequots took with them two young girls as hostages.

Four days later, a large party of the triumphant Pequots, traveling in many canoes, sailed past the fort at Saybrook. The Indians sang, shouted and waved over their heads the shirts of the men they had killed. In one of the canoes, Lieutenant Gardiner could see the two girls who had been taken captive. Gardiner fired the fort's cannon at the canoes, but the shots fell into the water and the Indians swept into the Sound.

Later it was learned that they had headed eastward to the Rhode Island coast and there tried to persuade the Narrangansett Indians to join with them in their war on the white man. Roger Williams, whose gentle manner had already won him some influence among the Narrangansetts, managed to persuade those Indians to ignore the Pequots and send ambassadors to Boston instead, to make a treaty with the English. The Pequots were not too disturbed. They were ready to fight the white men even without allies.

An emergency meeting of the General Corte was held in Hartford on May 1, 1637. The attack on Wethersfield could have only one answer. There was a unanimous resolution for "an offensiue warre against the Pequoitt." A draft of ninety men was ordered, a large number considering that there were fewer than eight hundred English men, women and children in the Three Towns at this time. Provisions for the men were ordered from the Three Towns, each town to contribute a certain amount of corn, one half of it to be baked into biscuit "if by any meanes they cann." Captain John Mason, an army man with a brilliant record of fighting for England in the Netherlands, now lived in Windsor. He was appointed commander of the troops.

Word was sent to the Bay Colony that war had been declared against the Pequots, and troops to help the Connecticut men were requested. But long before that plea for aid had been received, the colonists gained another important ally. The vengeful Uncas, seeing an opportunity to march against his rival, Sassacus, joined the English forces, along with about seventy of his Mohegans.

Thomas Hooker was no gentler than any other man when he saw his countrymen slain by the savages. The English and Indian forces gathered to set off on their expedition against the Pequots on May 20, 1637. Hooker stood before them and prayed for their success. "Our enemies have slain Thy servants . . . ," he said, "may our enemies fall like the leaves of the forest."

The English sailed off down the river. The Indians followed by land. They met at Fort Saybrook. There they were delighted to find the two young kidnaped girls from Wethersfield, who had been recaptured from the Pequots by a Dutch trading vessel. They were pleased also by the information the girls gave them about the arms the Pequots had and the scouts who were spying constantly on English activities.

After hearing about these scouts Captain Mason decided to try to give the Pequots the impression that the English forces had been frightened off. Instead of moving directly inland to Pequot country from the fort, the English, and Uncas with his Mohegans, boarded ship and sailed out into the Sound. Then they headed eastward. When they passed by the entrance to the Pequot River (now the Thames) Pequot scouts decided that the English were afraid to attack them and had passed on to meet easier foes, such as the Block Island Indians.

It was the impression Mason wanted them to have. Landing at Narragansett Bay, he went ashore with his forces and marched to the village of the Narragansett sachem, Miantonomoh. Mason asked Miantonomoh's help in attacking their joint enemies, the Pequots. Miantonomoh said the English forces were too small. When he learned that reinforcements were coming from Massachusetts, he wanted Mason to wait for them. But Mason was eager to press on while the Pequots still thought he was on his way to Block Island or some other place in that direction. At last Miantonomoh agreed that Mason and his men could march through his territory to attack the Pequots from the rear. A few Narragansett Indians joined the expedition on their own, partly to act as guides, and partly to satisfy their curiosity about what was going to happen.

Mason and his men, Uncas and his, marched westward overland, leaving the ship to follow them along the coast. At the end of the second day's march, when the forces were near the present town of Stonington, Mason called a halt. The Narragansett guides said they were near one of the two great Pequot forts. The other one, the chief residence of Sassacus, was a march of several hours farther on. Camp was made. Outposts could hear dimly the sounds of merriment somewhere in the distance. Before dawn, June 5, 1658, the men were on the march again. They came to a swelling hill (still known as Pequot Hill, near Groton). Uncas told Mason that the Pequot fort was on the top of the hill and that the Narragansett guides had fled to the rear of the little army out of fear.

"Tell them not to fly," Mason said, "but stand behind, at what distance they please, and see now whether Englishmen will fight."

What the watching Narragansetts saw was a fearful spectacle of how Englishmen could fight when determined to wipe out an enemy. Their forces were divided into two groups to scale the hill at some distance from each other. All was silence above. After the celebrations of the night before the Pequots were still asleep in their wigwams. The English and the Mohegans crept closer to the top of the hill, and a dog began to bark. A Pequot warrior stirred a little in his sleep.

"Owanux! Owanux!" (Englishmen!) he murmured. But no alarm was raised. Mason and his men, Uncas and his, tore down the piles of brush which served as gates to the fort and swarmed inside. The Pequots still were not fully aroused so the invaders rushed into the wigwams on either side of them and fell upon the Indians within. Soon there was hand-to-hand fighting in many wigwams. Then, as the Pequots awoke to their danger, there were arrows flying at the English from the doors of other wigwams.

Destruction of the Pequots by the English.

"We must burn the wigwams," cried Mason. He touched a firebrand to the mats which covered a nearby hut. The fire was fanned by a rising wind. Soon it was spreading swiftly through the fort. The blaze was so high that the attacking party began retreating down the hill. Halfway down, the English stationed themselves to shoot any Pequots who tried to escape from the furnace that the fort had become. Pequot warriors were still trying to shoot their arrows, but the heat was so great that their bowstrings snapped.

Within an hour five hundred Pequot men, women and children were burned to death. Seven were taken prisoner. Another seven managed to break through the English lines to escape. Only two Englishmen were killed and twenty were wounded.

Mason and his men began making their way to the coast

and the ship that had followed them. They planned to put the wounded on board the ship to be carried back to Fort Saybrook while the unwounded made the trip by land.

As the English were departing, a party of Pequots from the second fort farther west appeared at the scene of the massacre. They began to shriek and tear their hair at the sight they beheld. The English, watching their lamentations over the fate of their friends and comrades, felt no sympathy. This was "offensiue warre," and the enemy were to "fall as the leaves of the forest." More Pequots arrived at the burned fort. Some began running after the English, shooting their arrows. A few Englishmen were wounded but as the colonists fired their muskets in return a hundred more Pequots were killed. Then about fifty of the English boarded their waiting ship and the rest proceeded overland to Fort Saybrook.

No Pequot was so foolish as to think that this was the end of the matter. Every Pequot knew that the English would not wait long before moving against Sassacus and the second fort. The Indians who had seen the destruction of the first fort returned to their chief and reported on the English strength. A long council was held. At last it was decided that the English were too strong for the Pequots to resist. A plan was made. They would burn their villages and crops and then move quickly and secretly to safer land along the Hudson, traveling along the coast which was free of English settlements except for Saybrook, around which they would detour.

The swift departure began and soon the second fort and all the area around it was deserted. One group of Pequots, unwilling to leave their homeland, dropped out and took refuge in a swamp. Not long after they did so, the English forces from Massachusetts, under the command of Captain Stoughton, arrived in the neighborhood at last. Some Narragansetts told the Massachusetts men where the Pequots were hiding. Stoughton found them and his troops killed all the men and captured the women and children to be sent back to Massachusetts as slaves. He then moved on with his forces to join Mason and the Connecticut men at Saybrook.

Mason had already learned of the Pequots' flight by the time Stoughton and his men joined him. He detailed most of the troops to board ship and follow the fleeing Pequots along the coast westward. A few of the English, however, joined Uncas and his Mohegans to follow the Pequot trail overland.

Uncas sighted some of the fugitives near what is now the town of Guilford. The fugitives took refuge on a cape of land. Uncas led a party of his braves down one side of the harbor. Another party of Mohegans advanced on the other side. The fugitives, pressed to the end of the land by one group, jumped into the water to swim across the harbor. As soon as they came ashore they were shot by Uncas and his Mohegans. A minor sachem was one of those killed. Uncas cut off his head and placed it in the branches of a tree. For years after that, this spot was known as Sachem's Head.

The main English sea forces now came ashore at the mouth of the Quinnipiac River (the site of the present New Haven). A Pequot prisoner had bargained for his life with the information that Sassacus and many of his warriors were hiding in some swampy land twenty-five miles to the west. The English forces marched to the swamp. When they arrived they found almost three hundred Indians gathered in the marshy waters. Some were local Indians whom the Pequots had forced to join them.

The English surrounded the swamp and called out demands for surrender, promising mercy to everyone who had not killed an Englishman. The local Indians and the women and children of the Pequot party slowly came out of the swamp. Only the strongest Pequot warriors remained,

Uncas and Miantonomoh.

knee deep in the water and weeds. A guard was thrown about the swamp as night came, and all through the darkness there was fitful fighting.

Morning came with a heavy mist. Under cover of the mist, some of the Pequots managed to break through the guard around them. Some were killed, some mortally wounded. About sixty escaped, among them, Sassacus, the sachem. Those who were taken prisoner were divided among the Connecticut and Massachusetts forces to be sold as slaves. The wampum, weapons and cooking utensils that were captured were also divided among the two English forces.

Later it was learned that Sassacus and those braves who

escaped with him did indeed make their way to the Hudson River. But there they were captured by the Mohawks who killed and scalped them all. The Mohawks then sent Sassacus's scalp to the English as a token that the white men did not need to fear that sachem any longer.

The war with the Pequots was over. It had not lasted through the summer, but the English had broken the power of the Pequots in Connecticut so that it would never revive again.

Uncas remained. Various Pequots who had not taken part in the war straggled to him in the next months and joined his Mohegans in acknowledging him their chief. He continued to be an ally of the English, although he was not especially reliable.

In the next years there were difficulties between Uncas and Miantonomoh, sachem of the Narragansetts, about which of them had authority over all the remaining Pequots in Connecticut and Rhode Island. They fought and Uncas betrayed Miantonomoh into English hands. Ultimately, Uncas was given the assignment to kill Miantonomoh.

But there were no more wars between Indians and white men in the Connecticut territory for thirty years and more. The ruthless tactics of Captain John Mason and his men had accomplished this for the new Connecticul Colony.

As a reward for service in this war, the General Corte gave each returning soldier twenty-eight acres of land. This is believed to be the first soldier's bounty paid to American soldiers.

The danger from the Pequots being ended, the colonists of the Three River Towns, Hartford, Wethersfield and Windsor, could now turn their attention to the way in which they would set up their local government.

IV. Democracy
in the Three Towns

"Take you wise men, and understanding, and known among your tribes, and I will make them rulers over you."

Thomas Hooker was speaking, quoting from the Bible, as he began his sermon. Before him, sitting on the plain, back-less benches which were the only seats in Hartford's Meeting House, were the members of Connecticut's General Corte. Every man present was almost breathless with attention. What Hooker said in the course of his sermon would be the deciding factor in what sort of plans would be drawn up for the colony's government. Everyone knew Hooker's feelings about the need for all free men to have a voice in that government. Everyone knew that Hooker was aware of what each man before him felt and thought. There had been many, many private talks and discussions between all the people present—conversations at odd moments between the hard chores of breaking land, cutting timber, building houses, preparing for war. Hopes, fears, prejudices, long-held stubborn opinions, had all been threshed over, and Hooker, with his generous, understanding spirit, had helped each man realize what he wanted more clearly.

Each man knew what he hoped for. Each man felt he knew what Hooker wanted. But would he be able to justify that desire by Biblical authority? To a group of Puritans, nothing was possible, however dearly desired, unless it was sanctioned by the Bible.

"Take you wise men . . ." Hooker said. And then he went on to say that "the choice of public magistrates belongs unto the people by God's own allowance."

His listeners must have breathed deeply. It was what they had dreamed of. One man, Henry Wolcott, Jr., of Windsor, began taking quick notes of what Hooker was saying. It was a Puritan habit to make records of sermons. This record, miraculously preserved, allowed future generations a glimpse of how Thomas Hooker first spelled out the principles of democracy in America.

"They who have power to appoint officers and magistrates, it is in their power, also, to set the bounds and limitations of the power and place unto which they call them," Hooker said—spelling out the principle of the limitations of power which was still being fought out in England between the king and Parliament.

"Reasons:" Wolcott's notes continue, "Because the foundation of authority is laid, firstly, in the free consent of the people."

And this was the first time this principle had been so clearly stated.

Hooker went on, eloquent and inspired, to tell of other reasons why the people had the power to appoint, and to limit the powers of, their officers. Eagerly, Wolcott made his notes. Then, at last, Hooker was concluding, according to the pattern of sermons of that time, with an exhortation.

"As God hath given us liberty, to *take* it."

The men in the Hartford Meeting House must have felt

Meeting at Hartford of men from Hartford, Wethersfield, and Windsor to draw up The Fundamental Orders.

great and quiet joy when Hooker finished. Their minister had made clear, and given Biblical sanction to, all the dreams and hopes that had prompted them to move, first from Europe to America, and then from the Bay Colony to the wilds of Connecticut.

At once they appointed a committee to draw up laws which would put Hooker's principles into practice. Roger Ludlow, lawyer and first governor of the Three Towns, was one of the members of the committee. John Haynes was another. He had been governor of the Massachusetts Bay Colony in 1635. His dissatisfaction with the church government there had led him to come to Connecticut with Hooker in 1636. Other thoughtful, educated colonists were part of the committee.

Seven months later the group was ready with a carefully and clearly worded document called The Fundamental Orders. There were eleven of these orders. In their essence, they provided that the authority of the government came directly from the people—not the church and not the king.

The town was to be the unit of government. Representatives for the general legislature were to be chosen from each town in proportion to its population. There was to be no taxation without representation. All free men who took an oath to be faithful to the state had the right to vote. New towns that might be established had the right to join the original three and live under the same government. The legislature, consisting of a governor, six magistrates, and representatives from each town, was to meet twice a year. The governor and magistrates were to be elected annually by a vote of all free men gathered in a general assembly.

On January 14, 1639, The Fundamental Orders were accepted as the basis of government for the colony by a general assembly of the colonists of the Three Towns.

Using the word constitution in its modern sense, that is, a permanent limitation of government's powers, these Fundamental Orders were the first written constitution in history.

Legend has given most Americans the hazy feeling that the Mayflower Compact, drawn up by the Pilgrims of Plymouth, was the first democratic document of the New World. Actually, the Mayflower Compact began with an acknowledgment of the king as the source of authority for all laws. Democracy came into the Compact only accidentally as it affected church members.

The Connecticut constitution, on the other hand, was deliberately democratic. Voting was not restricted to church members but proclaimed to be the right of all free men.

This system of government, so quietly set into motion in the Three Towns in 1639, showed in miniature almost the same system that would be adopted 148 years later for the government of the United States. The towns were the unit of political independence in the Connecticut constitution, reserving all powers not specifically given to the general legislature, just as the states would be units of independence under the federal government as outlined in the Constitution of the United States.

"In matters of greater consequences, which concern the common good, a general council, chosen by all, I conceive

. . . most favorable to rule." That was how Thomas Hooker saw it in 1639. His vision inspired a government that served the Connecticut Colony so well that it endured, almost without change, until 1818, twenty-two years after the founding of the United States.

The strength of the system had been proved long before that, however. Within a few years after the writing of the constitution, the Connecticut Colony absorbed the Saybrook Colony on the coast, founded with no idea of democracy, but only as a refuge for noblemen. Not so many years later, it also drew into its orbit a third settlement in the Connecticut territory—the New Haven Colony.

This new colony was still in the process of settlement as the Three Towns were drawing up their Fundamental Orders. And the ideas of government held by its founders were as different as could be from those of Thomas Hooker. In 1639 it would have seemed impossible to the men of New Haven Colony that they could ever have anything in common with the Connecticut Colony to the north.

V. New Haven Colony

There was an air of good fortune about the men and women who founded the New Haven Colony. They were Puritans and had known the usual difficulties that Puritans met in England. Their minister and spiritual leader, John Davenport, had been forced at one time to flee to Holland, like so many others. But by and large, they were people with money. Theophilus Eaton, a long-time friend of Reverend Davenport's and important as a leader and advisor, had been a wealthy London merchant. Many others in Davenport's congregation were rich men who had been merchants, shipowners, importers and exporters. When they left their profitable lives and businesses in England, they hoped to establish some sort of equally profitable ventures in the New World.

They arrived in Boston in July of 1637. There were fifty men in the group, but with wives, children, other relatives and servants, their total number was about two hundred and fifty. They were welcomed by the people of the Massachusetts Bay Colony, who were eager to have such solid citizens settle among them.

But John Davenport and Theophilus Eaton were not sure that they wanted to become a small part of the Massachusetts Commonwealth. They had visions of establishing a commonwealth of their own where *their* church would be the controlling force.

They heard talk of the Connecticut country to which so many Massachusetts people had removed only the year before. Then Massachusetts soldiers who had been taking part in the Pequot War began returning to Boston and the little towns around it. They talked of the country along the north shore of Long Island Sound, over which they had pursued the fleeing Indians, and they spoke of its beauty and fertility.

Davenport and Eaton thought that area might offer the sort of new opportunity they and their party were looking for. In the fall of 1637, Eaton and a group of men went on an exploring trip to scout out the Connecticut coast. They were especially pleased by the region around the mouth of the river that the Indians called the Quinnipiac or Long-Water-Land. The land looked workable and pleasant. The river's mouth provided a good harbor for shipping. A rude hut was erected and seven men of the group settled in to spend the winter. Eaton and the others returned to Boston to arrange for a move in the spring.

Excited by Eaton's reports, various Boston colonists decided to join the Quinnipiac venture. By the spring, the group was so large that two ships were required for the party. The ships set sail at the end of March, 1638. Bad weather with storms and headwinds delayed them, and the voyage to the harbor of the Quinnipiac took two weeks. The ships sailed up one of the little inlets, West Creek, made anchor, and at last everyone was ashore, being greeted

The first Sunday in Quinnipiac.

by the men who had spent the winter there. One of them was missing—a victim of illness during the cold, hard months. This hardly seemed a good omen but the new settlers tried not to be discouraged.

They were stepping forth onto land presumably claimed by the Dutch, but the Dutch made no protest against these new English arrivals on their territory. There was no trouble with the Indians either. The Quinnipiacs were a small and feeble tribe, eager to trade with the new-comers and endlessly fascinated by watching them at their various activities.

When the Reverend Dr. Davenport preached his first sermon in the new settlement on April 18, Indians stood in groups on the surrounding hills, watching as the minister took his stand under a large tree with the people gathered around him. Davenport's text had to do with the "tempta-

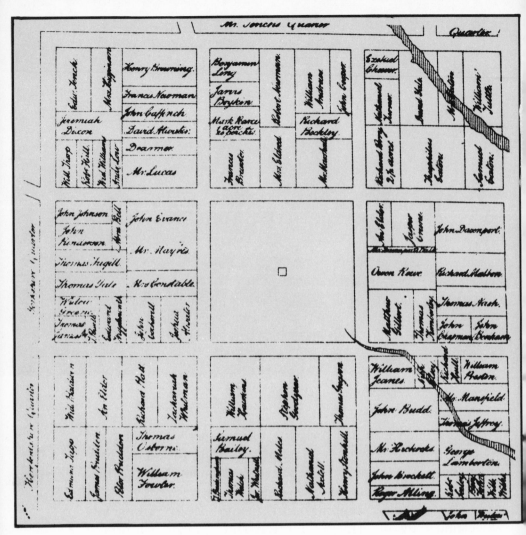

City plan of New Haven, Connecticut, in 1641.

tions of the wilderness." No record of what he said was left for history, but he probably spoke of the difficulties and fears in the new life that might tempt the settlers to give up.

Temptations to despair came soon enough. Spring rains washed out the seeds they planted, and it was necessary to plant all the crops again. But they went on with the practical matters of laying out the town and assigning land. The town, which was called Quinnipiac until 1640, when the name was changed to New Haven, was made half a mile square with a green in the center for a pasture and market place. Streets divided the remainder into nine equal parts. Lots for homes were assigned on the basis of money contributed to the venture and the size of each man's family.

The Reverend Dr. Davenport was given a large lot. Theophilus Eaton, the richest man in the colony, was assigned a large lot across the street from him. Other free men of the colony had lots of varying sizes around the square and then on beyond it to the limits of the town. Once land was assigned, everyone was busy from sunup to sundown, clearing land, felling trees, hewing timber and erecting shelters.

Another temptation to despair came on June 1, when an unlikely earthquake suddenly shook the whole area. The land trembled, the ships out in the harbor tossed on the waves and the water flung itself against the shore. The settlers fell to the ground and prayed. Finally, the tremor passed. The settlers arose and refused to give up. The work of building homes and a town went on.

In midsummer the colonists sent to Hartford for a certain Thomas Stanton, who could speak the Indian languages. Stanton arrived in early fall. Then the colonists built a great fire in the center of the green, summoned all the Indians from around about, and with everyone gathered around the fire, a council on buying land was held. With Stanton's help an agreement was worked out. The Indians granted the settlers the land around the mouth of the Quinnipiac River. In exchange they were granted an area to the east in which to live. The settlers granted the Indians hunting and fishing rights in the Quinnipiac area and promised them protection against the Mohawks. The English also gave the Indians some coats, spoons, hoes, hatchets, porringers, knives and scissors.

Before the council ended the English asked the Indians to stop doing some things that annoyed them. They should refrain, the English said, from wandering in and out of houses at will, from taking fish from the nets of the English, or using any boats that they saw unused, or from coming to trade on Sunday. The Indians could not see anything strange in this behavior, but when the English threatened to punish any Indians who persisted, they agreed to be more careful. In general, there were friendly feelings between the English and the Indians as the council ended.

Later that year, and during the next one, the Quinnipiac settlers bought more land in the area from the Indians. New parties of settlers arrived from England during that time, and they were settled on the new areas, forming the little towns of Milford, Guilford and Stamford—all part of the New Haven Colony. A tract of land on Long Island across the Sound was also purchased and another New Haven town called Southold was begun there.

Relations with the Indians continued friendly through all of this, but the New Haven colonists were not so foolish as to take safety for granted in the wilderness. Every man between the ages of sixteen and sixty was a member of the militia and required to have "a good, serviceable gunne, a good sword, bandaleers [a broad leather belt, worn over the shoulder and across the chest to support a musket] . . . one pownd of good gun powder, fower [4] pownd of bulletts . . . ," matches and flint. This militia, which was called the "train band," drilled and practiced target shooting on the green every Saturday morning. Seven men kept watch in the village every night to warn against fires or surprise attacks.

No elaborate plans for government were made in the beginning. Everyone was too busy. It was agreed that the laws of the Scripture would be followed. Theophilus Eaton was generally looked on as a judge to pass sentence on offenders. A whipping post and stocks were set up in the

The Reverend Dr. John Davenport.

green and anyone caught idling, stealing or drinking too much was likely to be sentenced to several lashes at the post or locked up in the stocks for a day or so.

Finally, by the summer of 1639, life had become ordered enough for the settlers at Quinnipiac to begin working out a more formal code of government.

A large barn belonging to one of the colonists was the meeting place for the colony's leaders. The Reverend Dr. Davenport opened the proceedings with a sermon.

"Wisdom hath builded her house; she hath hewn out her seven pillars," he began. From this text, Davenport was able to find Biblical justification for a form of government quite different from what Thomas Hooker had proposed to the men of the Three River Towns. Instead of a government in which all men took part, Davenport argued that the church—and the town—should be ruled by "seven pillars," or seven of its wisest men. Those seven pillars must necessarily be members of the church, and the ones who were to be the seven pillars could be chosen only by church members. Thus wisdom could build her house in New Haven, according to the Bible's directions.

There was some argument in the barn as one or two

colonists fought against a system which would bar any free man who was not a member of the church from any voice in the government. In the end they were defeated. "The Foundamentall Orders" as presented by the Reverend Dr. Davenport were adopted. Quinnipiac, soon to be New Haven, along with all the new little settlements under its jurisdiction, was as firmly committed as the Massachusetts Bay Colony to a government by the few, and those few only church leaders.

Twelve church members were chosen to select the "seven pillars" who would govern New Haven. Those twelve promptly chose Theophilus Eaton and John Davenport as the first two pillars. Then five more leading church members were selected. A few months later, in October, the seven pillars met as a general court. Eaton was elected magistrate. Four other pillars were deputies. Within a year or so, the magistrate's title would be changed to governor, but whatever the title, Theophilus Eaton held the office of the chief "pillar" for the rest of his life.

With church leaders and members firmly in control, the New Haven Colony soon began to develop a personality very much its own. Even more than in the Massachusetts Colony, every aspect of life was scrutinized from a religious point of view. And every offense, from murder to kissing on the street, was judged with the sternest rulings of the Bible as the authority. Almost half of the free men in the colony were not able to vote. There was no trial by jury, only by the magistrate and his deputies.

Still, there was no general dissatisfaction with life in New Haven for a long time. And the growing town continued to have an air of good fortune about it for some years.

VI. How People Lived
in Early Connecticut

The prosperity of the New Haven Colony, at least at first, was reflected in the houses of its two leading citizens. Theophilus Eaton, the richest man and the colony's governor, had a house built in the shape of an L. It was so large that it required nineteen fireplaces to keep it warm in the winter. Probably Eaton was not trying to show his importance with such a huge place. He had a very large family to shelter—his mother, his second wife, the children of his first marriage, the children of his second, various young people who were his wards as well as a number of servants. Altogether his household numbered thirty-two. Along with this large family, Eaton had also brought with him from England various household furnishings, Turkish carpets, tapestry hangings, carved furniture, brass andirons and other refinements. All these gave his house a look of unusual luxury.

John Davenport, who lived across the street, also had a

The first church erected in Connecticut was made of logs.

large house, built in the shape of a cross. It had thirteen fireplaces. Davenport's great luxury was his library, and he read and consulted his books so often that the Indians called him the "So-big-study-man."

The size and the appointments of these two houses were the exception, however. No settlers in Hartford, Wethersfield and Windsor in the Connecticut Colony had anything to compare with them. Certainly, most of the first settlers in all three of the colonies in the Connecticut area built and lived in much ruder shelters.

Legend has given us a picture of the early settlers in New England building log cabins as their first homes. Historians say this is probably not true. The English had no experience with that kind of construction. Coming from a land where timber was used carefully, they were accustomed to getting as much building material as possible from one log. It seems likely that the Swedes, coming from a heavily forested country, were the first to introduce log cabins into America with their settlement in Delaware. Later immigrants to the Middle West took the knowledge of that building technique with them to build log cabins in the backwoods.

The way the early Connecticut settlers did build came from a combination of what they knew from the past, what was available, the tools they had, and what they learned from the Indians.

The Connecticut Indians, for instance, often built round houses, as a home for one or two families. These were made by setting birch, ash or hickory saplings into the ground in a circle, ten to sixteen feet in diameter, with the tops bent together and tied with grape vines to form a dome-shaped roof. More saplings were woven or tied horizontally onto this framework, then the sidewalls and roof were covered with bark or mats plaited from flags or cattails. Longhouses, which held a number of families, were built on the same principle but in a long tunnel shape instead of a circle.

Some Connecticut settlers borrowed from this type of construction for their first temporary shelters, thrusting saplings into the ground as a framework. They generally shaped the shelter into a rectangle, though, and instead of mats, they covered the walls and roof with bundled thatch.

To picture them building more permanent homes, planting food, getting daily meals, clothing themselves and keeping warm in winter, one has to remember the pioneers of the Three Towns walking through the wilderness, driving cattle, sheep and pigs along with them as they traveled to the Connecticut area. They had no horses. Horses were not imported into the New England colonies until the 1640s. How much could they carry with them on such a journey? A few tools were vital. One plow, perhaps, that would have to serve the whole group for a while until more could be shipped from England or roughly made. Several spinning wheels were absolutely required for women to spin the wool of the sheep into yarn for clothing. Kettles and pans were also necessities. And all of these had to be carried by the pioneers themselves, or sent on small boats around the coast and up the river. The settlers of the New Haven Colony, going directly from Boston to their new home by ship, were able to carry a few more necessities but not many.

The wonder is how soon the Connecticut settlers did manage to create plain but solid buildings in the wilderness. In 1636, the very year that Hooker and his congregation settled in Hartford, the meetinghouse was built in which Hooker gave his famous sermon on democracy. It was a small, foursquare frame building, its walls covered by clapboards and its roof shingled.

To make the clapboards for the meetinghouse—or for any building—required a crosscut or rip saw and the labor of two men. A pit was dug and a log rolled across it. Then one man in the pit and one man above pushed and pulled the saw through the log, cutting it into planks. Shingles were a little easier to make. Logs were cut into short lengths and then split into thin sections. Many settlers covered their houses with shingles (or shakes) instead of clapboards. These shingles were so sturdy that many shingle-covered houses were in good condition a hundred years later. Still, even shingles took so much time to make that many settlers who covered the sides of their houses with shingles covered their roofs with thatch.

Nails, bricks, glass—items of construction that the colonists had taken for granted in England—were rare luxuries in the New World. Any that they had were brought from England until, with the passing years, the colonists found sources of metal for making their own nails, dug clay pits from which to make bricks, and established glass works. Most of the earliest settlers used wooden pegs for joining their constructions. Nails, which were made by hand even in England, were so rare that when used in building they were considered more valuable than the structure itself. If the house had to be abandoned for any reason, the owner burned it down to recover the nails. Instead of glass, the settlers used oiled paper or linen at the narrow openings

A New Haven scene of 1637.

they left for windows. Instead of bricks for their chimneys, they used logs chinked with clay at first. These caught on fire so often that they soon changed to stones mortared with clay.

Candles were also luxuries. Tallow, the necessary ingredient for making them, was not yet available to the early settlers because they could not afford to butcher very many of their cattle. For light at night, most people followed the example of the Indians and lighted pine knots. These knots were full of pitch and turpentine and burned with such a smoky flare, dropping so much pitch, that they were generally set on a flat stone on the hearth. Some of the settlers along the seacoast were able to use fish-oil lamps—even whale-oil lamps. Indians had hunted whale on the Sound long before the English arrived, and the English soon began whaling too. A fish- or whale-oil lamp was just a shallow vessel filled with the oil in which a wick was floated and then lighted.

It was no special hardship of the wilderness that houses had to be heated by and meals cooked at open fireplaces. That was how houses were heated and food was cooked everywhere in those years. But in the cruelly cold New England winters, the roughly built fireplaces did not warm much of the house, and they let in many freezing drafts. Baking would be much easier for Connecticut women when bricks were finally available so that brick ovens could be built, either beside the hearth or out behind the house.

The first and simplest food for the settlers was obviously the game of the region. Deer were so abundant in Connecticut that the men and boys of a family could quickly kill far more animals than were needed for meat. Often they simply left the carcass in the woods after stripping off the skin which was used in a number of ways. Wild turkeys and ducks and geese were plentiful and so were fish. The settlers along the river had fresh fish all summer long and could dry some for winter eating. Along the coast, the colonists could enjoy crabs, oysters, clams and lobsters. Following the example of the Indians, they learned to dry clams in the summer. Then in the winter they could add them to a favorite Indian dish that the settlers also ate often —succotash, a mixture of corn and beans.

The Connecticut settlers had the benefit of all that the Massachusetts pioneers had learned from the Indians about corn. They knew it would be one of their staple foods and drove their awkward plows into the ground to plant it as soon as they came to their new lands. After the corn had ripened, some was eaten fresh, but most of it was dried. The dried corn was ground down in wooden mortars to varying degrees of fineness. Cornmeal was used for flour, for porridges, for puddings, for dumplings, for a thickening or a base in almost any kind of dish. Potatoes were still unknown in both England and America at this time, and corn took the place of potatoes as well as of many other items. Pumpkins, beans and squash were other vegetables which the Indians had introduced to the Massachusetts settlers, and the Connecticut colonists planted them also.

Water was a drink of which most early New Englanders were suspicious. Beer, hard cider and wine were much preferred, and children drank them as well as grownups. But until the apple trees they planted grew mature enough to bear apples which could be pressed into cider, most Connecticut people had to make do with water. They found the water from the wells they dug generally sweet and fresh. Still they were glad when cider could be made. After that, pitchers of cider were on the table for every meal of the day.

Milk was not a very popular drink, and butter and cheese were rare until enough churns were brought over from England or handcrafted in the colony to enable housewives to make these dairy products regularly.

It was in the years after churns had become common that a Connecticut traveler wrote about a "playne supper but of exceeding relish," which he had eaten at a farmhouse. He had been served "warm rye loaves with butter and honey and bowls of sweet milk and roasted apples."

Coffee and tea were still unknown in England at this time, and so, of course, unknown to the Connecticut settlers. In the 1660s, the Dutch brought coffee to New York, and tea was introduced some time later. A packet of tea leaves found its way to Connecticut not long after that and completely mystified a housewife. She had no idea how to prepare this strange food and finally boiled the leaves, strained off the water, then served the stewed tea leaves with salt pork.

Men were busy building, farming, fishing, hunting. Women were busy spinning, weaving, cooking, baking. The children were busy, too. Not only did they have numberless small tasks to do at home, they also had school to attend. Puritans believed strongly in education so that everyone could learn to read the Bible. In 1641 the General Court of New Haven voted that a free school be started in that town.

*A Connecticut settler
and his family looked
something like this.*

The second school in Connecticut was started two years later in Hartford. Soon most towns of fifty families or more had schools.

Those first schools in Connecticut were only for boys who had already learned to read. They were called Master's Schools and the teacher was often the local minister. He taught the boys grammar, arithmetic and Latin, and intro-

duced them to the classics of literature. Little boys, and girls also, were expected to learn their letters at home. Soon, however, in most towns, some woman who had either the time or the energy took over the task of teaching a group of young children in her home. These schools for the youngest children were called Dame's Schools.

The clothing worn by the Connecticut settlers was sturdy

and simple. Men wore shirts and hose of homespun wool. Their trousers or breeches were often made of deerskin. Women's dresses were also of wool spun by themselves or made of some fabric brought from overseas. Imported fabric was generally called Holland fabric, whether it came from there or not. Buttons were made of wood, and hats were generally made of fur.

Silver buckles on a beaver hat, lace at the throat of a waistcoat, or a dress of silk on a woman, were not altogether unknown but the wearing of such finery was restricted to free men and their wives.

This privilege of dress accorded to "free men," added to the other far more important privileges such as the right to vote, brings up the question of who exactly qualified as a "free man" in Connecticut in those years. It is a puzzling one because what seemed perfectly clear to the colonists was not always recorded in a way to make it clear to later generations.

It would seem that in the New Haven Colony (as in Massachusetts) a "free man" was, first of all, a member of the Puritan Church in good standing. Secondly, he was an industrious and law-abiding citizen, and finally, but far from least—worth two hundred pounds either in money or investments. In the Three Towns of the Connecticut Colony, a "free man" did not have to be a church member. He did have to have a good character. And he did have to be worth a certain amount of money. Certainly it was taken for granted in all the colonies, and later in the United States, that only men of property could vote.

This business of making financial worth part of the test of a "free man" explains why so many pioneers to Massachusetts and Connecticut might well have been good Puritans but still be denied the rights of citizens. All kinds of artisans came to the new settlements from England. Carpenters, wheelwrights, blacksmiths and so on were all needed and valued members of the community. But if they did not possess the right amount of money or property they were not "free men."

Free men could vote and wear silver buckles. They were also the only members of their communities who were called "Mister." A man of no property was called "Goodman," and his wife was called "Goodwife," commonly shortened to "Goody."

Along with the aristocracy of "free men," and the lower class of "goodmen," there were other groups of men and women in the Connecticut colonies. The settlers in all the colonies brought indentured servants with them from England. These were young and old of both sexes who "bound themselves out" to a master for a certain number of years. During that period, they were more or less slaves of the master, receiving no pay. At the end of the time period, however, they were freed of their obligation and could establish lives of their own, becoming goodmen with little businesses or farms.

There was a slave class also in early New England. Puritan men and women, so obsessed by doing God's will, saw nothing wrong in owning other human beings just as they owned cattle, sheep or chickens. Indians captured in the Pequot war were sold to individual families as slaves. There were not many black people in Connecticut during the early years, but records show that a young Negro from Dutch Guiana was brought to Hartford in 1639 and held there as a slave. Later in the century, more and more black people, kidnaped in Africa, were brought to Connecticut and sold there as slaves. More than a hundred years passed before the Connecticut colonists began to question the morality of enslaving other human beings. Not until just before the Revolution did the colony pass a law prohibiting the importing of any more Africans as slaves.

The importance of money to being a "free man" was in

odd contrast, during these years, to what was *used* for
money in most everyday transactions. In many of these,
barter and exchange were an easier way for people to get
what they wanted than money would have been. When the
colonists bought land from the Indians, for instance, the
Indians far preferred useful items like hoes and knives to
English pounds, shilling and pence.

But even the Indians themselves sometimes had to use
some sort of money tokens. Their solution was wampum.
Wampum consisted of polished and carved beads made of
seashells, often strung on thongs. These beads were of two
colors, white, made from the inside of a conch shell, and
black (or bluish purple) made from the hard shells of
the hen clam. The black beads were considered more valuable since the shells were scarcer. For centuries before the
arrival of the white man, the Indians had spent much time
carving and shaping their wampum. Then the white men
brought steel tools which made the work much easier. The
shrewder Indian tribes at once began turning out great
quantities of wampum and became wealthy compared with
the less clever tribes. Connecticut settlers soon began making wampum, too, and they used it in various dealings both
with the Indians and with each other. It is recorded that
some settlers even put wampum in the church collection
plates on Sunday.

When the colonists were established well enough to
begin shipping items of trade back to England—timber, fish
and furs—the money situation became even more compli-
cated. England had a policy against paying in money for
any goods that came from its colonies. Instead, the colonists
were given credit against the purchase of any English manufactured goods they wanted to buy. This was part of what
was called the Mercantile System, which was followed by
most European nations in those years. It was based on the
theory that every nation should be as self-contained as

possible, relying on its colonies to supply needed raw materials and expecting the colonies, in return, to be a market for the nation's finished products.

During the early years of the American colonies, the system worked well enough. The colonists needed all sorts of manufactured goods. Later, toward the close of the century, it began to cause difficulties, especially for the New England colonies. England did not have as great a need for the raw material that came from them as it did for the tobacco, indigo and cotton that came from the southern colonies. Connecticut and Massachusetts really needed other markets for their goods, but English policies prohibited them from finding any. The pressures arising from this situation finally played a part in bringing on the Revolution against England.

But that was all far in the future. In the early years, the system chiefly meant that Connecticut colonists had little English money except what they had brought with them when they first crossed the sea and what was brought in by later arrivals. For a while, with all the other matters they had to concern them, that was enough.

VIII. Various Misfortunes

Ever since the Pilgrims led the way in 1620 there had been a swelling tide of Puritans arriving in America, fleeing England and the persecution of Charles I. In ship after ship they came, to increase the population of the towns already established, to start new towns around them, and to fan out into the wilderness where they founded new colonies and more new towns.

Sometime around 1640, the tide began to ebb. Fewer ships came bringing new settlers, but the new arrivals had news that could hardly fail to excite the colonists already in America. Charles I was running into difficulties himself. The members of Parliament had finally united to oppose his endless demands for money. And since many members of Parliament were Puritans by now, they were also insisting that he modify his behavior toward people of that faith. Puritans all over England were rejoicing at the stand Parliament was taking. But the king had his allies, too, who sup-

Lord and Lady Gardiner, from an old painting in the manor house.

ported him. Two parties were forming. The king's men were generally called the Cavaliers, while the Puritans and other opponents of the king were called Roundheads. Challenges and clashes between the two parties were coming more and more frequently. The stage was being set in England for a civil war between the Cavaliers and the Roundheads, but few of the American colonists could foresee what that war would mean to them.

Fort Saybrook, or the Saybrook Plantation, at the mouth of the Connecticut River, had been founded as a refuge for English noblemen who were Puritans. While John Winthrop, Jr., Saybrook's first governor, had still been in charge of the plantation in 1636, the wealthy and well-born George Fenwick came from England to visit the new settlement. Three years later Fenwick returned to take over the governor's post. This time he brought with him his new wife, Lady Alice Boteler, a troop of servants, various household furnishings and a few settlers for the colony. The party required two ships.

After Fenwick arrived, Lieutenant Lion Gardiner, who had commanded the fort from its beginning, took his leave.

He had purchased a small island just off the eastern tip of Long Island, giving the Indians ten coats of trading cloth for it. He called the island the Isle of Wight and there he went with his wife and small son, to build a home and live the rest of his life. (The island, now called Gardiner's Island, was inherited by his son, and after him, his son's son, and to this day is still the property of his descendants.)

At Saybrook, after Fenwick's arrival, a "fair house, well fortified," was built for him and his wife. Lady Alice planted flower and herb gardens. After the years of frontier monotony and Indian attacks, there was a mood of hope at Saybrook. More wealthy settlers were expected. Fenwick was sure that more pleasant homes and gardens would soon appear and that a rich town would arise on the land at the river's mouth.

Gradually the mood of expectancy at Saybrook began to fade. The wealthy friends and sympathizers who might have joined Fenwick and his wife were caught up more and more in the turmoil in England. Cavaliers and Roundheads were now meeting each other in battle. The fortunes of war were going first one way, then the other. Saybrook was not altogether forgotten in England. Puritans remembered it when things were going badly for them. According to legend, the Puritan soldier and leader, Oliver Cromwell, was once on board a ship ready to sail for America and Saybrook. The ship was delayed in sailing because of unfavorable winds. Then Cromwell decided against leaving England just then. He got off the ship and never made his way to America, after all.

The tumult in England went on and on. The Puritan lords and ladies who had once thought of moving to Saybrook were altogether taken up with the war. No new settlers came to Saybrook. Lady Alice gardened and made friends with the local Indians and nursed them when they were ill. She took care of the two daughters who were born to her and her husband. She rode horseback along the Connecticut shore—for horses had been imported to Connecticut from England at last. And Saybrook remained a lonely small settlement at the river's mouth.

Meantime, the New Haven Colony, westward along the coast, was bustling with new ventures. The men there had started shipbuilding almost as soon as they built their houses. Little New Haven vessels soon were making trading voyages along the coast and up and down the river, collecting furs, fish and timber. But to the enterprising businessmen of New Haven, it seemed that their trade could be improved. One of them, in the course of his voyaging, had come to the Delaware River. He explored it for some distance and then sailed home to report that the country along the river seemed to be very rich in furs and a good area for settlement. In 1640 the New Haven men sent an agent into that territory to buy a tract of land along the Delaware River from the local Indians.

That the Dutch and the Swedes already claimed the territory did not seem to bother the New Haven people. After all, the Dutch claimed the very land on which New Haven was built, and there had been no trouble about that.

Fifty families set off from New Haven for the Delaware River area, taking with them the various supplies necessary for starting a settlement. They chose a site near Salem Creek for their new town. Land was cleared. Shelters were built. Crops were planted.

Then, suddenly, the Dutch who had paid so little attention to English activity for several years, heard about the new settlement and were outraged. The Swedes in the Delaware area were equally angry. William Kieft, governor of New Amsterdam, who was known as William the Testy because of his irritable way with the Indians, sent off two ships filled with troops to Salem Creek. The soldiers attacked the Connecticut settlement, burnt the houses and took the settlers prisoner.

Now the New Haven men were outraged in their turn.

They had invested a great deal of money in the Delaware River venture. They thought the Dutch were far outside their rights in what they had done. They were determined to retaliate.

Just about this time the Massachusetts Bay Colony was suggesting to the other New England colonies that they form a union for mutual protection against the Dutch and the Indians. The Connecticut Colony had made just such a suggestion several years before, but no one was interested. Now New Haven was quite ready to be part of such a group. And so the New England Union, the first real alliance of several English colonies for their mutual benefit, was formed in 1643. Massachusetts, Plymouth, Connecticut and New Haven all sent delegates to its first meeting, and George Fenwick was asked to represent the Saybrook Plantation. That colony had little to contribute to the mutual defense, but Connecticut men had not forgotten that the Saybrook Colony was the only one in the Connecticut territory that held a royal grant to its land from the English king.

The first business to come before the New England Union was the Dutch attack on New Haven's Delaware settlement. A letter of protest was sent to William the Testy, but that had no effect. New Haven's delegates pressed the Union for more action, but the other colonies were not eager to back up New Haven's claims in Delaware by force. It seemed a bad time to tangle with the Dutch. They were fighting with the Indians just now in the area which later became the border between New York and Connecticut. During one of these skirmishes, Anne Hutchinson, the outspoken religious thinker who had been banished from Boston, was killed, along with her family. Most delegates to the New England Union were afraid that sending any troops into Dutch territory just now might turn the Indians against them as well.

New Haven's grievance remained unsettled. But the Union did show its value by settling an old dispute between Connecticut and Massachusetts about their northern border line.

Even more important, Connecticut leaders and George Fenwick became friendly in the course of the border settlement. Fenwick told the Connecticut men of the disappointment that the Saybrook settlement had become. The Connecticut men decided that this might be a good time to try to buy the Saybrook Plantation and the royal patent with its grant to such a wide sweep of American territory. They made Fenwick an offer for the patent and the plantation.

Fenwick probably found it a sad decision to make. But as things were in England, it was impossible to foresee a time when large groups of rich and noble Puritans would come to Saybrook. He sold Fort Saybrook and all the land in its neighborhood to the Connecticut Colony on December 5, 1644. The rest of the land which was included in the Warwick Patent—land which extended from Narragansett Bay to the Pacific—was also to be turned over to Connecticut's jurisdiction by Fenwick if it came into power to do so. Fenwick received a certain sum of money, the right to remain at Fort Saybrook for ten years and the right to tax all shipments of corn, biscuit, beaver and cattle that passed by the fort during the same length of time.

Massachusetts people were not very pleased by the news of the sale and were very annoyed by the tax which meant that shipments from their towns farther north on the Connecticut River would all be taxed when they came to the mouth of the river. They evened the score by imposing a tax on cargoes coming into Boston Harbor from Connecticut.

New Haven people had even more reason to be disturbed by Connecticut's purchase. If the whole Warwick grant ever should be upheld in Connecticut's favor, it would

Oliver Cromwell was a Puritan soldier and leader in England.

mean that Connecticut held jurisdiction over New Haven territory as well as Saybrook. There were anxious discussions in New Haven about what could be done.

While they worried, news arrived from England occasionally. The Puritan cause was meeting with more and more success. Cromwell was remodeling the army. The Puritan forces were moving with new vigor. Then in the summer of 1645 came the news that Cromwell and his New Model Army had won a stunning victory over the king's forces at Naseby.

The New Haven leaders suddenly began to consider this news in connection with their own problem. It was beginning to seem that the Puritan forces might finally triumph in England. In that event, Oliver Cromwell would be a man of great influence and power. And Cromwell was as good a friend of the New Haven Colony as he had been of Saybrook.

The plan that came to them then seemed as though it might not only help them gain a safeguard for their territory but also recoup some of their losses from the ill-fated venture on the Delaware.

All the men in the colony with money to spare pooled

their resources. They had been building small ships on
their own beach for years, but for this venture they wanted
a large ship. They ordered one from a shipyard in Rhode
Island.

The "Great Shippe" was what they called the new vessel
in their records. It could hold one hundred fifty tons of
cargo, and when it arrived at New Haven the colonists
loaded it with every kind of goods that could be profitably
traded in England. Several passengers were also going to
make the voyage to England. Chief among them was a man
appointed to meet with Oliver Cromwell and ask him for
his help in getting the New Haven people a sound and legal
English title for the land which they had bought from the
Indians and on which they had built their towns.

Everyone was so eager for the mission to be under way
that it seemed impossible to wait for good weather. The
ship was ready in January of 1647. It was so cold that the
harbor had frozen over. Gangs of men broke the ice to
make a passage for the ship. Then the sails were raised, the
wind filled them, and the ship moved slowly out of the
harbor. On the shore, a prayerful crowd watched and
waved as the "Great Shippe" grew smaller and smaller to
the sight and then vanished over the horizon.

Naturally no one expected news of the ship for some
time. People did not really begin to worry until six months
had passed, and there was no word at all of her and her
passengers. Other ships from England touched briefly at
New Haven. Those on board had no news of the "Great
Shippe." Hope in New Haven began to change into fear.
Then, as still more months passed, fear turned into grief.
The "Great Shippe" surely must have been lost, and with
her all the friends, relatives—and goods too—that were
aboard her.

The rest of the story became legend in the New Haven
Colony. A year and a half passed. It was June of 1648. A

The house that Thomas Hooker lived in in Hartford, Connecticut.

great thunderstorm blew up on a hot afternoon and swept over the town, then on across the Sound to Long Island. An hour later, just at sunset, when the air had that strange clarity that often follows a storm, someone gasped at an unbelievable sight. He called others and pointed. At once a crowd gathered, with everyone growing more excited by the moment.

The "Great Shippe" was out there on the Sound. She was moving swiftly in from the horizon toward the mouth of the harbor, seeming to float on a cloud on the surface of the water. Soon everyone could see every detail clearly, the riggings, the catwalks, the carving on the bow. Joy welled in every heart. Then it was noticed that only one man was on deck. He was leaning on his sword and looking sadly toward the group on shore. A hush of awe and fear fell over the crowd. Then, as the ship came very close, everyone saw a fearful shudder pass over her. The masts blew away, the hull capsized. Suddenly the whole vision disappeared in a mist. Then the mist itself was gone.

The stricken people turned to their minister, John Davenport. Davenport gave them the only explanation he could think of for the vision they had seen. God had sent the phantom ship of the air to show them how their friends and relatives who had been aboard had perished.

There were those who thought of giving up the whole New Haven venture after this. Some talked of emigrating to Ireland, others spoke of the island of Jamaica. But gradually, such talk died down. People in New Haven began to pay a little more attention to farming as a way of life, but they continued to dream of some grand business scheme that would restore their vanished fortunes.

In the Three River Towns of the Connecticut Colony, life had gone on with few alarms during these years. Thomas Hooker had died in 1647, and the colony mourned him. But he had left his legacy of democratic ideals and by now the colony continued to practice them in a quiet, taken-for-granted sort of way.

In 1648 (the same year the phantom ship appeared at New Haven), Lady Alice died at Fort Saybrook. George Fenwick buried her on a hill near their home. Soon after that, he returned to England, long before his ten-year lease on the settlement had expired. Before he left, Hartford leaders urged him to remember the Warwick Grant while he was in London and make every effort to make sure the Connecticut Colony did indeed have jurisdiction over the vast territory it defined. Fenwick promised to do so, but when he arrived in England the Civil War was coming to its climax. The Puritans were triumphant everywhere. The king was in custody and was going to be tried by a panel of sixty-seven judges. In times of such fantastic happenings, who was interested in questions about an old, half-forgotten grant?

Charles I was be-headed in 1649.

Charles I was brought before his judges. In his hours of desperation he was quiet and dignified, answering the charges against him in a reasonable way. The judges were not moved. They arrived at their decision—a decision that astonished all of Europe and sent shock waves through the American colonies, too, when the news arrived there. On January 30, 1649, Charles I was beheaded.

It still did not mean the end of the Civil War in England. Charles's son was now proclaimed King Charles II in Scotland. Cromwell and his army had to rout the Scottish army and the supporters of Charles II in two battles. Finally Cromwell was victorious, and in 1653 he had supreme power in England and was named its Lord Protector. The Puritans and Protestants who had been harried and persecuted thirty years before were now the ruling class of England.

The Puritans of New England, who had given up so much and suffered so much to gain a way of worship that was now the one approved way in their homeland, must have pondered the irony of fate. But few thought of returning to England even though Puritanism was triumphant there. Their hearts were given to their new homeland by this time, and their energies were engaged in meeting all the challenges it presented.

VIII. Defying the Dutch, and Other Excitements

The Dutch, to the west, seemed a constant threat to the people of Connecticut and New Haven, and the threat suddenly grew much greater when New Amsterdam acquired Peter Stuyvesant as its new governor. Stuyvesant, a fiery man who stumped around on one good leg and one wooden peg, appeared determined to press Dutch claims in the Connecticut territory as no earlier Dutch governor had done.

Actually, the Connecticut people did not need to become quite as agitated as they did. The Dutch West India Company, which backed Holland's ventures in America, had no intention of letting the New Netherlands colony tangle with the much stronger New England colonies in any kind of war. All Stuyvesant's appeals for men and money to back the Dutch claims by force were refused.

But then Stuyvesant decided to present his Connecticut claims in person. He appeared in Hartford in September,

1650, when the New England Union was meeting there. Firing off a letter to the delegates in which he demanded recognition of Dutch rights, he headed the letter "New Netherlands," taking it for granted that Hartford was part of his colony.

The delegates were not taken in by that trick and refused to accept the letter. Stuyvesant then backed down on his claim to Hartford but wrote again, asking for satisfaction. After an exchange of letters—Stuyvesant insisted that all the negotiations be in writing—it was agreed that a committee be appointed to determine the exact extent of Dutch holdings in the Connecticut territory. Stuyvesant was allowed to choose two of the committee members.

Connecticut people had every reason to be pleased—and Stuyvesant every reason to be disappointed—with the committee's findings. The Dutch were to remain in control of the land around their trading post, the House of Hope, near Hartford. Aside from that, the committee granted the English authority in the Connecticut territory westward to within ten miles of the Hudson River. They were also awarded the greater part of Long Island. Stuyvesant really had no choice but to sign the treaty which affirmed these boundaries and stump back to New Amsterdam.

New Haven men felt so encouraged by all this that they decided to make a new try at settlement on the Delaware River land from which the Dutch had driven them several years before. Fifty families joined the expedition. They boarded a ship loaded with supplies and set forth. The confident captain of the ship then decided to stop briefly at New Amsterdam.

The sight of the English ship in his own harbor, bound for land in his territory, was like the last straw to the frustrated Stuyvesant. He flew into a towering rage and had everybody on board the ship arrested. They were released only when they promised to return at once to New Haven.

The English and Dutch often quarreled in Connecticut.

Stuyvesant then sped them on their way with many threats of what would happen if they made any more attempts to settle on the Delaware.

With no thought of having done any trespassing themselves, the men of the New England Union wrote a strong letter to Stuyvesant and warned him that they were prepared to defend any Delaware settlement that New Haven made.

Hard feelings between the English and Dutch in America were encouraged by hostilities between the English and

Dutch overseas. When Cromwell came into power in England, the Netherlands refused for more than a year to recognize him, preferring to greet the son of Charles I as king of England, even though he was in exile in Europe. Finally the Dutch grudgingly accepted Cromwell as England's leader, but there was so much trade rivalry between the two nations that English and Dutch ships were constantly engaging in battle on the sea.

When news of those naval battles reached the Connecticut colonies, Connecticut people were even more distrustful of their Dutch neighbors. Rumors began to fly that Stuyvesant was inciting the Indians in the western part of the Connecticut territory, near the town of Greenwich, to rise against the English. These rumors were easy for Connecticut people to believe for it was in that area that Anne Hutchinson and her family had been massacred a few years before.

An ultimatum was sent to Stuyvesant to stop inciting the Indians. Stuyvesant, outraged, replied that he had done no inciting. A committee was appointed to investigate. No proof was discovered that Stuyvesant was plotting with the Indians, but the Connecticut people were convinced he was, even so.

The matter came before the New England Union. The Connecticut people wanted to declare war on the Dutch without delay. The Massachusetts delegates hesitated and then refused to vote for war. The disagreement was so serious that the strength of this first union between New England colonies was greatly weakened.

Connecticut and New Haven men decided to proceed with preparations for war without the support of Massachusetts. The militia began drilling and supplies were collected. Connecticut people were much encouraged when Cromwell decided to support their cause. A small fleet from England arrived in Boston to help the colonists in their attack on the Dutch at New Amsterdam. After the fleet

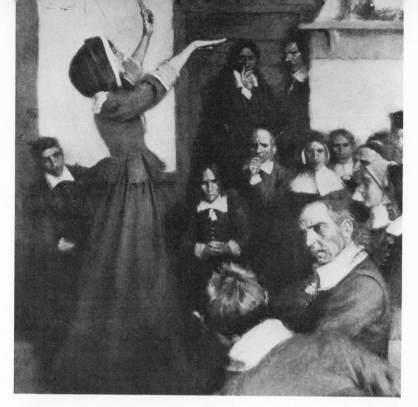

Anne Hutchinson preaching in Boston.

appeared, Massachusetts agreed reluctantly to begin enlisting troops from its territory.

But before any forces could set out against New Netherlands, news came that England and Holland had signed a peace treaty. New England, in its turn, had to give up its designs on New Netherlands. Cruelly disappointed, Connecticut men refused to give up without at least a token gesture. They marched on the Dutch trading post near Hartford and seized it. With the English holding the House of Hope, the Dutch lost their last outpost in Connecticut territory.

After that, an uneasy sort of truce existed between the English and Dutch for a few years. The men and women of both the Connecticut and New Haven colonies went their various busy ways, farming, fishing and improving their towns and their lives.

Charles II.

And then, once again, events in England had their echoes in America. Oliver Cromwell died. For a while his son, Richard, attempted to carry on the Protectorate established in England. But Richard Cromwell had none of his father's talents as a leader. As a result, those Englishmen who had never ceased supporting the royalist cause began to work actively to bring back from exile the son of the beheaded Charles I.

It was July of 1660 when a ship landed at Boston and brought the news. A royalist army had marched on London in the beginning of the year. Charles II had landed at Dover in April. The Puritan Commonwealth had ended. The monarchy was restored with Charles II on the throne.

The news spread swiftly into the Connecticut territory, bringing with it a wave of concern. The colonists there had been left to go their own way almost completely during Cromwell's years of power. Few new settlers had joined them, but on the other hand, few English decisions had interfered with what they wanted to do.

People were somewhat reassured to hear that Charles II was ascending the throne in a spirit of tolerance toward the Puritan faith and would not punish in any way those who had rebelled against and fought his late father.

Still, there had been two noteworthy passengers on board

the ship from England. They were Edward Whalley and his son-in-law, William Goffe. Both of them were lawyers, and both had been members of the panel of sixty-seven judges who had condemned Charles I to death. However forgiving Charles II might be, few of those judges (who were called regicides, or king-killers) wanted to press his generosity beyond its limits. Some had fled to the continent after Charles II's coronation. Whalley and Goffe had chosen to come to America.

At first the people of Boston greeted the king's judges as distinguished guests. Then came word from England that Charles II had indeed pardoned most of his father's enemies, but he could not forgive the men who had condemned his father to death. Warrants were out for the arrest of all the regicide judges. Whalley and Goffe decided to leave Massachusetts and disappear into the Connecticut territory.

They arrived first in Hartford where they were made welcome but soon they journeyed on to New Haven. There the Reverend Dr. Davenport greeted them and installed them in his home as honored guests. Whalley and Goffe made no attempt to hide but moved freely about the town. Both were experienced soldiers, and they helped the train-band drill on the green each Saturday.

Then officers of the king, with warrants for the arrest of Whalley and Goffe, arrived in Boston.

It did not take Dr. Davenport long to decide which way his path of duty led. If he had to choose between obedience to the king or aid to Puritan fugitives, the Bible helped him make the decision. On Sunday, he preached a sermon on the text, "Hide the outcasts, bewray not him that wandereth." His congregation understood the message, and all were ready to help however they could.

Whalley and Goffe appeared later dressed as though for a journey. They set off in the direction of New Amsterdam and walked all day. When night fell, they turned around and made their way back to Davenport's home. There they hid in the cellar for the next month. After that, they hid in the cellar of the house across the street for another month.

The king's officers made their way into Connecticut, stopping to make inquiries at Hartford. The people of Hartford were no more anxious to betray the fugitives than the New Haven people. But Hartford men seemed to have a talent for taking the practical course. They had no desire to offend the king's officers or, ultimately, the king, and so they made a great show about sending out proclamations and warrants. But they made sure at the same time that their efforts would accomplish nothing.

The king's officers pressed on toward New Haven. At Guilford, one of the towns of the New Haven Colony, they were delayed by the New Haven governor. First, the governor insisted that their credentials be read aloud in a town meeting. The next day being Sunday, the governor insisted that nothing could be done until after the Sabbath. As these obstacles were raised, one after the other, an Indian runner was sent on to New Haven to warn Davenport that Whalley and Goffe were in danger.

By the time the king's officers finally made their way to New Haven, Whalley and Goffe were in a woods outside the town. They hid for a while in an old mill. Then they made their way to a cave near the summit of a large hill known as West Rock. For more than a month they hid in that cave (which is called the Judges' Cave to this day). A farmer who lived not far away brought them food whenever he could. They were frightened by storms, and once a panther threatened them at the mouth of the cave, but they managed to scare it away.

Then they learned that Davenport and other New Haven leaders might be in jeopardy for protecting them. They decided to go down into the town and give themselves up. But they reckoned without the loyalty of the New Haven people who insisted that they return into hiding. For a while longer, Whalley and Goffe stayed in the cave. Then they began a time of wandering. For days, or weeks or months, they stayed sometimes in New Haven, sometimes in Milford or Guilford and sometimes in Hartford. And they continued to evade capture by the king's men.

Finally, in 1664, special royal commissioners arrived from England with orders to search Connecticut for the regicide judges. Whalley and Goffe left the Connecticut territory which had protected them for four years and made their way to a little town called Hadley, in western Massachusetts. There they were taken in by a minster who sheltered them for the rest of their lives. Whalley died in 1674 and Goffe five years later.

Still another regicide judge found sanctuary in Connecticut. In 1664, just as Whalley and Goffe were leaving the territory, one of the judges, whose name was John Dixwell, arrived in New Haven. He said his name was James Davids, and he protected his disguise so well that no one guessed his true story. He married and raised a family. Gradually, he became friendly with a minister and told him his secret, and so when Dixwell, or Davids, died in 1689, his true identity became known. Still, his gravestone was marked "J.D., Esq." "Lest his enemies might dishonor his ashes." (The old stone may still be seen behind the Center Church on New Haven Green.)

Meantime, while the people of New Haven were adding excitement to their lives by hiding and befriending the king's judges, Hartford men had seen another sort of opportunity now that Charles II was on the throne. They were quickly seizing it.

IX. Connecticut's
Wonderful Charter

The Connecticut Colony had decided it was time to appeal to the king for a charter that would guarantee both the government its founders had established and the territory that its settlers had purchased and fought for. Why it had not made such an appeal to Oliver Cromwell and why it acted as though Charles II would be more sympathetic is hard to know. It could not have been only because John Winthrop, Jr., owned a ring that Charles I had once given to his grandfather, which might, for that reason, arouse kindly feelings in the king. It might have been because John Winthrop, Jr., was now governor of the Connecticut Colony.

Winthrop was a most unusual man. He had been governor of Fort Saybrook for a year in 1636. After that, he had gone to Fisher's Island, off the northeastern tip of Long Island, and built a home for himself and his family. He had also begun the pioneering development of America's natural

Nevv-Haven's
Settling in
NEW-ENGLAND.
AND SOME
LAWES
FOR
GOVERNMENT
Published for the Use of that Colony.

Though some of the Orders intended for
present convenience, may probably
be hereafter altered, and as
need requireth other
Lawes added

LONDON

Printed by M. S. for Livewell Chapman, at the
Crowne in Popes head Alley
1 6 5 6.

*A year before John Winthrop was elected Governor of
the Connecticut Colony, Governor Eaton drew up a set
of laws for the New Haven Colony.*

resources that he would continue all his life. On Fisher's Island he built a small plant to secure salt by boiling sea water. Later he spent some time in Massachusetts and England in connection with the mineral resources of Massachusetts. He followed that up by establishing ironworks in two Massachusetts towns in 1644. He then was given authority by the Massachusetts government to establish a settlement in the old Pequot country, along the banks of the river now called the Thames. (Massachusetts claimed this territory because of the help its troops had given Connecticut during the Pequot war.)

Several Massachusetts families had moved with John Winthrop, Jr., and his family to a site near the mouth of this river. They founded the town later called New London. Here John Winthrop built a new home. He also built the first grist mill in the country, which used water power to grind corn and wheat and to saw timber.

He was hardly settled in this new region, however, before the New England Union awarded that particular territory to Connecticut instead of Massachusetts. A "free man" of Connecticut now, Winthrop soon became one of the colony's magistrates and in 1657 he was elected governor. His talents were so obvious, and so necessary to the colony, that its people voted to change the rule prohibiting the reelection of a governor. John Winthrop, Jr., was reelected year after year after that.

So John Winthrop, Jr., was governor in 1661 when the General Court decided it was time to send a representative to the new king in England, offering him Connecticut's allegiance, and also asking him for a royal charter.

A petition was drawn up that detailed much of Connecticut's history—the trading with the Indians, the war with the Pequots, the purchase of Saybrook and the Warwick grant, the arguments with Massachusetts about boundaries and the difficulties with the Dutch. The petition then asked the king to help Connecticut define and maintain its borders and protect its government by granting it a charter.

To make sure the charter would contain just what was wanted, the Connecticut court drafted a sample one for the king. John Winthrop, Jr., was then chosen as the colony's representative, and in midsummer of 1661 he set sail for England. With him, he had the petition, the sample charter, all sorts of documents including parchments signed by the Indians, a letter to Lord Say and Sele (who was a friend of the new king), five hundred pounds for expenses and the ring that Charles I had given his grandfather.

Good fortune followed Winthrop in all his efforts in England. Lord Say and Sele was ill but gave him letters to other noblemen who could be helpful. Winthrop met the Countess Castlemaine, a pretty lady who was one of the king's favorites. She was so entranced by stories about the Indians and by the Indian documents that Winthrop had that she promised to use her influence with Charles in Winthrop's favor if he would just give her one of the parchments signed by the Indians. What with one thing and another, Winthrop was soon in the presence of the king himself. The king was well impressed by this intelligent and courteous petitioner from far-off Connecticut and touched by the gift of the ring that had been his father's. He promised to study the petition and charter that Winthrop laid before him and all the other documents that supported it.

On April 23, 1662, Charles II signed the charter just as it had been drafted by the Connecticut General Court and affixed to it the Royal Seal of England. In the charter he granted to the Connecticut Colony all the lands covered by the Warwick Patent, or a strip of land as wide as Connecticut and extending from the Narragansett River to the Pacific Ocean. This plainly included the New Haven territory and simply ignored Dutch claims.

Even more important was the kind of government the king granted to the Connecticut Colony with the charter. In the years since its granting, many historians have marveled at the freedom and independence Connecticut won. The historian George Bancroft, who was first to write a full history of the American colonies, called the charter "extraordinary" and went on to write:

> It conferred on the colonists unqualified powers to govern themselves. They were allowed to elect all their own officers, to enact their own laws, to administer justice without appeals to England, to inflict punishments, to confer pardons, and in a word, to exercise every power, deliberative and active. The King, far from reserving a negative on the acts of the colony, did not even require that the laws should be transmitted for his inspection; and as no provision was made for the interference of the English government in any event whatever, Connecticut was independent except in name.

Winthrop reported the success of his mission in a letter to the colony which arrived there in midsummer of 1662. He wrote simply that the charter had received the great seal and that it was "as full and large for bounds and privileges as could be desired."

He sent the charter itself by a later ship since he had to stay on in London and get a duplicate charter signed and sealed. The original charter was shown first to the New England Union commissioners who were meeting in Boston. The men of New Haven, reading it, must have pondered on the future of their own colony.

In October the charter was in Hartford, where it was read aloud to an assembly of the free men of the colony. It was announced that the document belonged to them and their descendants forever.

After the reading, the charter was given for safekeeping

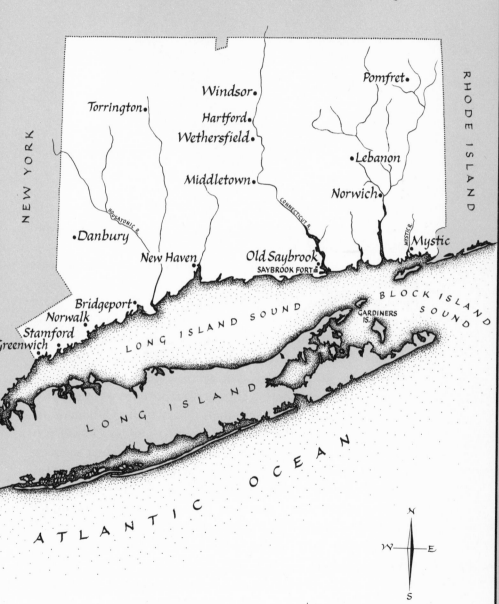

The Connecticut Colony in the Colonial Period

Peter Stuyvesant.

to three men, Samuel Wyllys, whose father had been the third governor of the colony, Captain John Talcott and Lieutenant John Allyn.

There was no doubt that the Connecticut colonists were proud of the document and what it meant to them. Some twenty-five years later, when it seemed they might have to give it up, the crisis brought about one of the most romantic incidents in Connecticut's early history.

Right now, however, Connecticut's leaders were not thinking of future perils but were eager to put the provisions of the new charter into action. Letters were sent out to all the towns that were included within Connecticut's boundaries under the charter, asking them to choose representatives to attend a general assembly and so become part of the Connecticut system. Milford, Guilford, Stamford, and Southold on Long Island—all the little towns that had been part of the New Haven Colony—responded promptly, not unwilling to be members of a colony so much more democratic than what they had known.

Only in New Haven itself was there resistance. The Reverend Dr. Davenport, still firmly committed to a colony governed only by church members, dug in his heels. He could not bear the thought of the colony for which he had struggled so long becoming just another town under Connecticut rule with the power of the church taking second place to ordinary civil rule.

For two years the struggle went on. Davenport and other New Haven leaders resisted every effort of the Connecticut Colony to take it over. But all the while there was a growing number of free men in New Haven who were becoming convinced that the old system must go and the new one take its place.

Then, as so often before, events in England triggered a decision in America.

The Merry Monarch was what people called Charles II, referring to his pleasure in music, the theater and gay companions. But he seems to have had a merry, almost whimsical, approach to some of his royal decisions as well. In 1662 he had signed the charter for the Connecticut Colony, granting it east-west boundaries from the Narragansett River to the Pacific Ocean. In 1664, two years later, he suddenly made a gift of land to his younger brother James, Duke of York and Albany. The gift was a sweeping grant of American territory that covered all of Long Island and the mainland from the Connecticut River to Delaware Bay. This, of course, took in all of the New Netherlands territory and that part of the Connecticut territory which included both New Haven and Hartford.

The news of this astonishing grant came to America in July, 1664, when a fleet and an army from England arrived in Boston on their way to move on New Amsterdam and capture it from the Dutch. By August the English fleet had carried out its assignment. Stubborn old Peter Stuyvesant held out for a few days, but he really had no choice. New Amsterdam was surrendered to the English and renamed New York, in honor of its new sponsor, James, Duke of York. Dutch territories up the river were also surrendered to the English, and the Dutch trading post a hundred miles up the Hudson was renamed Albany, also in honor of James.

The situation was alarming enough to Connecticut people. Land which they had thought was theirs had been given to someone else. There seemed little that they could do, however, except carry on under the terms of their charter of 1662 and see what happened.

For the people of New Haven the moment of decision had come. They had no royal charter at all to the territory they claimed, which had now been granted to both the Connecticut Colony and the Duke of York. Faced with the choice of having to submit to one or the other, New Haven could not help feeling that it preferred to join with Connecticut. Connecticut's leaders had been generous in their offers of granting New Haven people equal security with their own. They had promised that all past quarrels and difficulties would be "buried in perpetual silence."

At last even John Davenport accepted the decision to join Connecticut. Grieved by the end of what he had fought for, he did not stay long in New Haven but soon moved to Boston, where he died in 1670.

Meantime, when the Connecticut General Assembly met at Hartford in March, 1665, deputies from all the former New Haven towns were present. Four former New Haven leaders were chosen as magistrates in the Connecticut government. But New Haven had ceased to exist as a separate colony. The influence of the church would continue strongly in the New Haven area for years, but its actual political power was gone. All the towns in the Connecticut territory were now under Connecticut government.

X. Hiding the Charter

The English had been settled in Connecticut for almost thirty years now, time enough for a generation of children to be born, grow up and start families of their own. And in spite of all the upheavals that had been caused by the Indians, the Dutch or events in England, life had its everyday patterns that were busy, peaceful and more and more civilized.

Farmers had been working to such purpose in the rich bottom lands of the Connecticut valley that Connecticut had become a granary of New England. Wheat, corn, peas and beans from Connecticut were shipped to Boston, New York and to England as well, often in ships from Connecticut's own yards. Fishing fleets were busy on the Sound, bringing in great hauls of fish for drying and exporting. Whaling ships from Connecticut towns were ranging farther and farther asea.

Exports to England had enabled the colonists to obtain

in exchange many more of those tools and furnishings that made life more comfortable. And many men had followed the lead of John Winthrop, Jr., building mills along rushing streams where falls or dams could provide water power.

In the routine of life, there was even time for gaiety now and then. Dancing and card playing were frowned upon in Puritan Connecticut, but people gathered at house- or barn-raisings, at quilting bees, apple harvests and husking bees, and enjoyed gossip, jokes, flirting and laughter. Tobacco and liquor were both in wide use, so much so that Connecticut magistrates were often busy passing laws against their abuse. Tobacco was a crop that grew well in Connecticut, but liquor was imported from England. Trade with the West Indies, which would one day supply the colonies with great quantities of rum, had not really begun.

If there was uncertainty about the exact legal state of Connecticut's claims to its territory, it was not something people worried about every day. The Duke of York seemed to be paying no attention to his Connecticut rights, so for several years there were no special alarms.

Every day, in most Connecticut towns, a town crier walked up and down the streets, beating a drum to attract attention, and then crying out the news. The events he announced might be only local births or deaths or marriages, the date of an auction or cattle sale, the arrival or departure of a ship; but this was the news of everyday life that interested everyone.

Many towns had inns or "ordinaries" by now, where travelers could get food and lodging for the night. Travelers were always welcome for they brought news from other parts of the country. But around 1669 and 1670 Massachusetts travelers began bringing news from their colony that was not so welcome.

Massachusetts was again worrying about the Indians.

The Indian sachem around whom their fears centered was one of the sons of the great chief Massasoit, who had been a good friend of the Pilgrims. He had been so friendly with the English, in fact, that he gave his two sons English as well as Indian names. They were Alexander and Philip. After Massasoit died, Alexander became chief. Then Alexander died under curious circumstances. His brother Philip became sachem and gradually Philip came to believe that the English had poisoned Alexander. Outwardly, Philip and the English in Massachusetts were still at peace, renewing vows of friendship every year. But there were signs of growing hostility toward the English among the members of Philip's tribe, rumors that the Indians wanted revenge for Alexander's death.

Connecticut people were bound to be concerned by such news. As members of the New England Union, their militia would have to march to the aid of Massachusetts if war broke out, and besides no one ever knew how far trouble could spread when Indians began attacking. Everyone was much relieved in 1671 to hear that King Philip, as the English called him, had been summoned to answer to charges of conspiracy and had cleared himself with what seemed like great sincerity.

Astonishing news came from the colony now called New York in 1673. The Dutch had recaptured the colony on Manhattan Island and given it back its old name, New Amsterdam. Connecticut did not have long to worry about new threats from the Dutch, however. The very next year troops from England recaptured the colony on Manhattan Island and firmly renamed it New York, the name it would keep from then on.

But James, Duke of York, had now been aroused to paying more attention to the English territory in America which his brother had given him. He got a new grant from his brother and then appointed a royal governor to

Sir Edmund Andros.

come to America and take jurisdiction over the former
Dutch territory and the region between the Connecticut
and Delaware rivers as well.

Sir Edmund Andros, the new royal governor, arrived in
New York in 1674. Shortly after that, the Connecticut
Assembly heard that he planned to take over the government in every part of the Connecticut territory claimed by
the Duke of York's charter.

All through the winter and spring of 1675, Connecticut
people worried about how they could preserve the independence that had been theirs since 1639. Then in June
their troubles were compounded. King Philip suddenly
led his Wampanoags in a surprise attack on the town of
Swansey, in Massachusetts, killing eight of the inhabitants.

Word of this attack, along with a plea for troops, reached
Connecticut just about the time that word came from New
York that Sir Edmund Andros was on his way to Fort Saybrook with a force of men. In his message, Andros said he
was coming to Connecticut to help with the Indian
troubles, but no Connecticut man or woman thought
that was his only reason.

The Connecticut colonists did not yield to panic. A
certain number of the militia, under the leadership of
Major Robert Treat, were called out to march to the aid of

Massachusetts. At the same time, another practiced soldier, Captain Thomas Bull, was ordered to Fort Saybrook with two companies of men.

Bull's orders were worded so that he had authority to resist any attempt to take the fort, whoever made it. He was told that if Andros appeared he was to inform him that the colony had already taken precautions against the Indians and needed no help. Andros was to be directed to the actual scenes of conflict. Bull was not to permit any armed soldiers to land.

> And you are to keep the king's colors standing there, under his majesty's lieutenant, the governor of Connecticut; and if any other colors be set up there, you are not to suffer them to stand . . . you are in his majesty's name required to avoid striking the first blow; but if they begin, then you are to defend yourselves, and do your best to secure his majesty's interest and the peace of the whole colony of Connecticut in our possession.

The day after Captain Bull arrived at Saybrook, two sloops sailed into the harbor. Soon Sir Edmund Andros was coming ashore along with a party of his men. They advanced toward the fort under the flag of the king. But the flag of England was flying over the fort as well, and Andros could hardly order his men to fire on that. He frowned, then ordered an aide to read aloud the duke's charter and his own commission as governor. Bull and the representatives of the Connecticut government said that this had nothing to do with them. They withdrew, ordering their troops with them. Andros had the charter and commission read even so. Then, as if he was not sure just what else he could do, he and his men departed.

Andros had not given up. He was determined to assert his authority in Connecticut and he returned to New York to bombard the colony's leaders with letters ordering them to bow to the duke's command.

Meantime, the war known as King Philip's War was continuing its bloody course in Massachusetts. The Indians, remembering the destruction of the Pequots, made only one raid into Connecticut territory, and though they burned several homes they killed no one. But more than three hundred Connecticut men and a hundred and fifty of their Mohegan allies were fighting in the war. Many were killed in Massachusetts, trying to help their fellow colonists and protect their families at home. The thought that the Indians were also fighting to protect *their* families and the land and way of life that had been theirs for centuries never seemed to occur to the English.

They wasted no sympathy on the capture and death of a brave young chief of the Narragansetts, Canonchet, the son of the chief Mianomotoh. When Canonchet was sentenced to death by the English, he said, "I like it well. I shall die before my heart is soft, and before I have spoken anything unworthy of myself."

The English finally captured King Philip's wife and son whom he dearly loved, and sold them as slaves in Bermuda. When Philip heard this news he bowed his head and said, "My heart is broken. I am ready to die."

The war was almost over in any case. The combined forces of Massachusetts, Connecticut and Rhode Island had killed hundreds of Indians. Finally Philip retreated with a few followers to a hill in Rhode Island where the graves of his ancestors were. There one of his own men, whose brother Philip had killed for advising peace with the English, killed the sachem. It was August, 1676, and the death of Philip marked the end of his war. His head was cut off and carried to Plymouth. The English there saw nothing barbaric in placing it at the top of a pole as a warning to all Indians of English vengeance when attacked.

The death of King Philip.

This was the last great war between the English and the Indians in New England. Later, they would fight each other many times, but the Indians would not be fighting on their own but allied with some other enemies of the English, often the French.

The end of the war did not mean any end of Connecticut's difficulties with Sir Edmund Andros. These dragged on and on. Somehow, by always responding patiently and courteously but never missing or yielding on any favorable technicality or point of law, Connecticut managed to stay free of his authority.

Andros finally was recalled to England in 1682. The new English governor in New York proceeded to negotiate with Connecticut about the boundary between that colony and New York. This was a reassuring project for Connecticut people who did not mind losing a town or two on their western border so long as they had the boundary.

Then, in 1685, Charles II died. James, Duke of York and Albany, became James II of England. He was not very popular in England. He had converted to Catholicism, a religion many English people feared or distrusted. He had engaged in various plots that seemed to favor Catholics. Still, he had let his daughter, Mary, marry a Dutch Protestant prince, William of Orange, and no one had protested when James took the throne after the death of his brother. But new troubles for Connecticut and all New England began almost at once.

James had a plan that seemed very logical to him. He would unite all of England's colonies in the northern part of North America under one government. Defense against the Indians, the Dutch, the French, too, would be much easier to provide under such a system. Commerce, trade, taxes, law enforcement would all be simpler. To anyone who had not lived and worked his way through the various differences in faith and personality that had separated the

New England colonists into their several territories, nothing about the plan seemed unreasonable.

Sir Edmund Andros was appointed the new governor-in-chief of all New England.

He was returning this time with authority that was going to be impossible to resist.

Arriving in Boston in December, 1686, Andros sent out letters to all the general courts and assemblies of Massachusetts, Rhode Island and Connecticut. He requested that their charters, patents or grants be turned over to him at once so that the new central government might be inaugurated at the king's command.

Reluctantly, Massachusetts and Rhode Island obeyed. But their charters were not the hard-won documents of democracy that Connecticut's was. Connecticut leaders did not know what to do. They could not refuse the king's command, but whom could they send to plead their cause with the king's governor? John Winthrop, who had been so eloquent in earlier years, was dead. The governor now was Robert Treat, the strong, blunt man who had led the colony's forces in King Philip's War. It seemed to Governor Treat that all Connecticut could do was delay in handing over its charter. Delay, and delay, and delay, hoping something would happen to change the situation.

Connecticut managed to delay for over a year. Then Andros left Boston to visit Hartford in person, accompanied by a troop of seventy soldiers. He arrived in Hartford late in the afternoon of All Hallows Eve, October 31, 1687. The militia was drawn up before the Meeting House to give him a proper military welcome. Governor Treat waited before the building to escort him in. The colony governor and the royal governor greeted each other in a courteous manner.

What happened during the rest of the afternoon and evening has become part of Connecticut legend, and there are many versions of the story. Most versions agree on some basic facts.

The hour being late, Governor Andros asked Governor Treat and the Connecticut representatives to join him for dinner at the inn across the green. After dinner it was suggested that Andros and the Connecticut men hold their conference in an upstairs room of the inn. Two candelabra, holding fourteen candles, were brought for light. The meeting began. Andros spoke quietly but ended by demanding the charter. Governor Treat spoke about what the charter meant to Connecticut, but finally he had to produce it.

He snipped the deerskin thong that held the rolled parchment. The document half unrolled itself across the table. There was some more talk about how precious it was to Connecticut and how much effort, blood and money had gone into achieving it. One of the older representatives, a man named Andrew Leete, who had been ill for some time, got up to speak. He talked with growing emotion. Then, suddenly, he fell forward across the table, unconscious. As he fell, his arms knocked over both candelabra and all the candles were extinguished. The room was in darkness.

By the time the candles were lighted again the charter was gone.

According to legend, the charter had been handed, under cover of the darkness, to a young captain of the militia who was standing next to a bay window. This young man, Joseph Wadsworth, stepped quickly through the open window, onto the stairs outside it and then ran down them and into the night. He evaded the English soldiers of Sir Edmund's guard, crossed the little "riveret" that ran through the town just there and made his way to the home of Samuel Wyllys, one of the original guardians of the charter.

A great oak tree stood in front of the Wyllys house. It was the same oak that the Dutch captain Adrian Block had seen when he sailed up the Connecticut River in 1614. It

The Charter Oak at Hartford, Connecticut.

was the oak under which the Suckiaug Indians had smoked
their peace pipes, the oak that signaled the time to plant
corn when its leaves were the size of a mouse's ear.

The tree was old now, and there was a hollow in it.
Captain Wadsworth took off his soldier's tunic, wrapped it
around the charter, and thrust the package deep into the
hollow of the great oak. Then he ran off into the darkness.

Back at the inn, Sir Edmund did not allow himself any
bad temper when it was seen that the charter was gone. He
had come to force Connecticut men into a position where
they must either surrender their charter or resist the king
openly. He had failed in both goals. The charter was gone.

The Connecticut leaders had not resisted him.

An entry was made in the records of the General Court:

At a General Court at Hartford, October 31st, 1687, his
excellency, Sir Edmund Andros, knight and Captain General and Governor of His Majesty's territories and do-
minions in New England, by order of His Majesty James
the Second, King of England, Scotland, France and Ireland, the 31st of October, 1867, took into his hands the
government of the colony of Connecticut, it being by His
Majesty annexed to Massachusetts and other colonies under
His excellency's government. Finis.

In other words, the Connecticut authorities had submitted to the government of Sir Edmund Andros as they
were forced to do. But they had not surrendered their
charter.

Connecticut was not happy under the rule of Andros.
Neither were the other New England colonies. Andros
probably was not the villain that Connecticut legend has
painted him. He was simply a hard-working colonial officer
trying to carry out the orders of his king. Fortunately, those
orders did not last very long.

James II, who had not been popular to begin with,
managed within four years to outrage his subjects so completely that they forced him to abdicate the throne. His
daughter, Mary, who had married William of Orange, was
brought back from Holland to rule the country along with
her husband.

The news of the bloodless Glorious Revolution came
to New England in the spring of 1689. James II was de-
posed. William and Mary were the new rulers in England.
The authorities in Boston hurried to clap the hated Andros
into jail. In Hartford, Connecticut, the authorities quietly
began functioning again under the terms of the charter that
had never been surrendered.

James II.

A few years later, John Winthrop, Jr.'s son, Fitz John Winthrop, was sent to England to confirm the terms of the charter. All the best lawyers agreed that the charter had been granted under the royal seal. It had not been surrendered under the common seal of the colony, nor had any judgment been rendered against it. As one English lawyer said: "Its operation had merely been interfered with by overpowering force; that the charter therefore remained valid."

It remained valid through all the next century and some years into the one following. The great oak in the hollow of which the charter had been hidden remained even longer. It fell during a storm on August 21, 1856. Botanists tried to estimate its age from the rings in its trunk and decided it was almost one thousand years old. The wood of the fallen tree was carefully preserved. Three elaborately carved chairs were made from the wood and are still on exhibit in Connecticut.

XI. Witches,
Colleges and Wars

Bad went along with good. People had clear vision about some things, but they also had blind spots. These were the years when good Puritans who had fled persecution because of their religious beliefs were themselves persecuting Quakers for their faith. New Haven was harsher about this than Hartford. Any Quaker who wandered into New Haven was likely to find himself imprisoned in the stocks for a day or so.

These were also the years when people became obsessed by a fear of witchcraft. They believed a person could sell his soul to the devil and would than have the power to do all sorts of mischief. A particular wave of terror swept across New England in the 1680s and 1690s. When anything unusual happened—when a child became ill, or butter would not churn, or a cow died unexpectedly—people looked for the witch who was responsible. Any odd or eccentric old woman might be suspected. Sometimes suspicion fell on a young woman of whom the town was distrustful. Some women became hysterical when accused and confessed to all sorts of unlikely things. Some denied everything. It really made little difference when the witch-hunting fever struck. There were trials, presided over by ministers and magistrates. There were tests. Sometimes an accused witch was thrown into the water. If she floated she was guilty. If she drowned, she was innocent, which judgment was not of much use to her any longer. Those whom the juries found guilty without the water test were generally hung.

Massachusetts suffered more from the witch-hunting fever than Connecticut did, but Connecticut had its share of hysteria, accusations, trials and executions.

In contrast to this unreasonable behavior was the founding of a college in Connecticut. John Davenport had begun planning for a college in New Haven almost as soon as the town was founded. In 1648 the General Court had appointed a committee to reserve some land for a college building. But New Haven's misfortunes with its Delaware colony and the lost "Great Shippe" had not left it enough money to go ahead with the plan. Massachusetts liked to think that Harvard College in Boston, established in 1645, served as a college for all New England. Each New England colony was asked to contribute to its support. A certain amount of corn was sent to Harvard every year from Connecticut and called "college corn."

Still Connecticut did not give up hope of its own college. Finally, in 1701, the General Court passed an act for the establishment of a collegiate school wherein "youth may be instructed in the arts and sciences who thorough the blessing of Almighty God may be fitted for Publick Employment both in Church and civil State." The new institution was called a "collegiate school" so as not to attract undue attention from the English king. It was "so low a name that it might better stand in wind and weather."

A witchcraft trial in Connecticut.

Ten clergymen met and donated books for the library of the new college. Forty books were collected, a measure of how few books there were in the settlement sixty-five years after its founding.

Saybrook was chosen as a site for the college since it was easy to reach by water from both New Haven and Hartford. However, the first and only teacher was a minister who lived in the town of Killingworth. His congregation did not want him to leave, so classes were held at his home in Killingworth for several years. Later some classes were held in Milford. But a real college could hardly begin to operate in such a disorganized way. Finally, after a good deal of wrangling between New Haven and Hartford, New Haven was chosen as a permanent location for the college.

A Connecticut man named Elihu Yale, who had made a fortune in the East Indian trade and then retired to

England, had been interested in the college plans from the beginning. When he donated a generous sum, the first real college building was erected in New Haven in 1717. It was three stories high and painted blue. In honor of its benefactor it was named Yale College.

Before long the college began to grow and prosper and lay the foundations for the great university it later became.

During these years the Connecticut colonists were also called on to do their share in one war after another. These wars reflected the various conflicts that England was having with both France and Spain. But for the colonists they seemed chiefly directed at stemming the growing power of the French in North America, who suddenly seemed much closer and more dangerous than ever before.

Actually, of course, the French had been exploring and setting up forts and trading posts in North America since Jacques Cartier discovered Newfoundland in 1535 and then went on to find and enter the St. Lawrence River. The French were not settlers to the degree the English were. Like the Dutch they were interested in the fur trade. Also, most Frenchmen who came to America were adventurous spirits who loved exploring the wild rivers, lakes, forests and mountains of the northern part of the continent. Samuel Champlain discovered the large lake in northern New York that still bears his name. Louis Joliet and Père Marquette began exploring the Great Lakes and the great inland rivers of the continent. Then Robert Cavalier, Sieur de La Salle, rode the wide waters of the Mississippi in a canoe from the Great Lakes to the Gulf of Mexico.

In a very large, loose sort of way, the French were encircling the English coast colonies with forts and trading posts to the north and west. There were not nearly so many French in America as there were English—only about 12,000 French as against 215,000 English in 1690. But

Colonists fought in various wars in the 1700s.

the French, though spread out over thousands of miles, were more united in spirit than the English, who were divided into twelve different colonies, each jealous of its own authority. Even more threatening to the English were the good relations which the French had with the Indians. The French had little of the racial prejudice that the English had. They looked on the Indians as their brothers, worked with them, helped them when they could, and many Frenchmen married Indian wives. As a result, the French could count on a great number of Indian tribes as their allies in any war. This increased their strength against the English out of all proportion to their actual numbers.

In history books, the wars that erupted periodically in

America through the 1700s have names that read like a roll call of the English sovereigns who happened to be reigning when they were fought: King William's War (1689–97) ; Queen Anne's War (1702–13) ; King George's War (1744–48). To the colonists who fought in them they all seemed to be wars against the French and Indians and forerunners of the war that lasted from 1758 to 1760, which even the history books call the French and Indian War.

The first war (King William's) was triggered by an attack of the French and Indians on the town of Schenectady in northern New York. Connecticut sent troops to help defend the town. Connecticut also sent men under the command of Fitz John Winthrop to take part in a land excursion up the Hudson River. These land forces were supposed to cooperate with a force coming by sea to take the French city of Quebec. The expedition failed.

In the next war (Queen Anne's) the English once again hoped to capture Quebec and also sent an expedition against the fortified French city of Montreal. Neither city was taken. But the English forces, Connecticut men among them, did manage to win the island of Nova Scotia from France, which was a great blow to France's old and warloving king, Louis XIV.

Another little war, without a kingly name, came next. This was the War of Jenkins's Ear which was fought between 1739 and 1742, mostly in the southern part of America. The settlers of the new colony of Georgia bore most of the brunt of that conflict, which was caused by a quarrel between England and Spain. But cooperation between the English colonies in America was becoming more reliable. Connecticut sent a thousand men to take part in an English expedition against Cartagena, a Spanish city in South America. The expedition was defeated with great losses. Only a hundred Connecticut men returned home. Some of them may have become acquainted during the expedition with a Virginia captain named Lawrence Washington. After the English defeat, Captain Washington went back to Virginia where he became a soldierly inspiration to his young half-brother, George. Certainly, in all these expeditions, whether they were failures or successes, men from the different English colonies were getting to know each other.

The next war (King George's) focused on the great Louisburg fort which the French had built on the island of Cape Breton. The fort was planned to overlook and control all sea traffic to the northern shores of North America. Eleven hundred Connecticut men took part in the assault against this "Gibraltar of America." The fort was supposed to be impregnable, but for some reason the four thousand New Englanders who took part in the attack against it looked on the assault as a "mad frolic." With this attitude, they managed to win the fort and returned home rejoicing. They felt a good deal let down later, when England made a peace treaty with France in 1748 and returned the Louisburg fort to French control.

They felt even more dismayed when a new war between England and France began to loom before six years had passed. There were reasons to fear that this time even greater numbers of Indians would be fighting with the French.

The alarm was so great that seven English colonies made a move toward cooperating for their mutual defense. This was a much larger group than the New England Union had been. All seven colonies sent delegates to Albany, New York, for the first congress ever held by so many colonies acting together. The hope was that they could work out a joint treaty with the Iroquois Nation of Indians so that all seven of them could rely on the Iroquois as allies in the forthcoming war. Among the delegates to the Albany Congress were many men who would help make history

The fall of Braddock.

twenty years later. One of the most outstanding was a Philadelphia printer, Benjamin Franklin, who had a plan for the colonies to join in a permanent union for their own defense, creating a general government with a president-general and a grand council.

Oddly enough, it was the Connecticut Colony with its long history of expanding democracy within its own territories and its long membership in the New England Union which refused to accept the idea of a general colonial union. Its leaders feared having their own control over the militia given to another authority.

The Union plans of the Albany Congress faded and soon after that the last great French and Indian War began. England sent a professional army man, General Edward Braddock, to lead the colonial forces against the French Fort Duquesne (later Pittsburgh). Braddock's second in command was a young colonial from Virginia, George Washington. Washington warned Braddock about the possibility of an Indian attack. Braddock scoffed at the idea of Indians attacking the king's regulars. Soon after that the troops were ambushed by Indians. Braddock was mortally wounded, many others were killed. Washington took command and arranged for an orderly retreat that saved the army from ruin. Three years later, with Washington assisting another English general, John Forbes, Fort Duquesne was taken.

The same year that Braddock was ambushed, Connecticut troops were with General Wolfe when the Louisburg fort on Cape Breton was taken again from the French and this time destroyed. In 1759 Connecticut men took part in the capture of another French fort. This one stood where Lake Champlain and Lake George met. The French called it Fort Carillon and the English called it Ticonderoga.

Once Ticonderoga was won, a waterway was open to Canada. At last English and colonial troops managed to capture Quebec. A Connecticut man from the town of Pomfret, Israel Putnam, was one of the colonial officers who aided General Wolfe in this victory. The next year, 1760, Montreal was captured by English troops, commanded by General John Jeffery Amherst.

With these English and colonial victories, the power of France in North America was broken completely. When peace was made this time between England and France, France gave up all her territory in America except New Orleans and two small islands south of Newfoundland.

Before the war ended, England also became involved in fighting the Spanish in the West Indies, who had been trying to aid the French. Connecticut sent a thousand men to help in the Caribbean, among them Colonel Israel Putnam, who had fought at Quebec. The English were finally successful in the West Indies also. They won Havana as well as the islands known as the Lesser Antilles. But thousands of men died, many of them from disease.

By the end of this last struggle, Connecticut leaders were feeling somewhat differently about the idea of union with other English colonies in America. Men from all the colonies had fought side by side in the cold of Canada, the wilderness of the west, the heat of the West Indies. All the colonies had spent what amounted for them to a great deal of money in supplying and outfitting the men who served. They had helped the mother country, England, to win the continent by their mutual efforts. Many of them had the feeling that they were the ones who had won the continent, with a little help from England.

XII. Connecticut Yankees

The Land of Steady Habits was one name that other colonies had for Connecticut by this time. The kind of quiet, day-to-day democracy that was practiced there seemed to encourage men to have sturdy, responsible characters.

Yankee was what people were beginning to call a man from Connecticut, or any New Englander. Historians are not sure just where the word came from. One theory is that it was adopted from the Dutch *Jan Kees* (or John Cheese), which was pronounced Yan-kees. Considering the years of distrust between Connecticut and New Amsterdam, it is odd that Connecticut people came to be called by a Dutch name. Still, by 1760, colonists all up and down the eastern seaboard were using the term Yankee and knew exactly whom they meant by it—a New Englander, and especially somebody from Connecticut.

Certain traits, along with steady habits, were associated with Yankees. People from the middle and southern colonies thought of Yankees as practical and shrewd, quick to make a good bargain, quick to invent ways and means of doing things in a simpler, easier way.

These were the years when peddlers began traveling from town to town and colony to colony selling items that were not easy to get in the little stores that had been established in most towns. At some harbor town like New Haven or Boston or New York, peddlers bought pins and needles and mirrors, spices and coffee and silk and lace. They packed their wares in bundles that they carried on their backs, or stowed them in carts that they pulled by hand. Then they went forth along the roads and paths that led past lonely farmhouses to little villages in the backwoods. Housewives always welcomed the peddlers and were thrilled to get some small luxury which only they provided. Probably no more Connecticut men went out as peddlers than men from other colonies, but people generally spoke of "Yankee peddlers."

The fabled shrewdness of Yankee peddlers was responsible for a Connecticut nickname that endures to this day. Among the spices peddlers carried were nutmegs, walnut-sized nuts which could be ground into a delicious flavoring for apples. Nutmegs were grown only in the East Indies, off the coast of Asia, on islands owned by the Dutch. The Dutch were responsible for importing almost all the nutmegs that were available in Europe and America. But according to colonial folk tales, peddlers from Connecticut were so crafty that they carved replicas of nutmegs out of wood and sold them for the real thing. A "wooden nutmeg" was the same symbol of being cheated as a "wooden nickel" became in the next century. Connecticut, supposedly the home of the sharp practice of making wooden nutmegs, is still known as the Nutmeg State.

Tall tales like this probably helped neighboring colonists express a certain jealousy of the enterprising men of Connecticut. The soil of Connecticut, which had seemed so fertile at first, had finally proved not so rich after all. The many hills, with stony outcroppings, limited the amount of farming land that was available. And the population of Connecticut kept growing. By 1760 almost two hundred thousand people lived there, and there were seventy-three towns. But this shortage of good land seemed to act as a challenge to Connecticut people. If they could not make a living by farming, they turned to the mills on their many rushing rivers and started small industries. They made useful items needed in other colonies. They invented things.

During the French and Indian War a boy named John Fitch was growing up in South Windsor, tinkering with various crafts, working as a clockmaker, a silversmith and a gunsmith. Later, after the Revolutionary War, John Fitch built the first successful steamboat in America, a steamboat that ran regular passenger runs on the Delaware River seventeen years before Robert Fulton's steamboat was tried out on the Hudson River off New York.

Clockmaking was a promising new industry in Connecticut. In later years some of the best-known clocks in America came from that region, made by such famous makers as Eli Terry, Seth Thomas and Chauncey Jerome. Later, also, the inventor Eli Whitney would settle in New Haven, and with his invention of the cotton gin and his theory of mass production, he would do much to change the course of life in America.

A newspaper was started in Hartford in 1764, *The Hartford Courant*. It was not the first newspaper in the colonies, but because it never suspended publication it became the oldest continuously running newspaper in America.

Boys were growing up in Hartford who would later make their names as poets. Noah Webster was born in West Hartford in 1758. He grew up to be a man fascinated by

Noah Webster.

words and published a spelling book that sold more copies than any book except the Bible.

Trade with the West Indies was in full swing by this time, adding many luxuries to life in Connecticut. It had begun, so far as Connecticut was concerned, about 1690, when Captain Samuel Chester sailed out of New London, his little ship loaded with a cargo of flour, barreled pork and salt codfish. He sailed to one of the islands of the West Indies, and there he found sugar planters eager for just such items—cheap food for the slaves they kept to work their plantations. Two months later, Chester was home again with a cargo of sugar, molasses and a cask of rum. Connecticut's West Indian trade had begun.

The trade was not always within the letter of the law as laid down by England's Navigation Acts. Colonial ships were only supposed to trade with English ports. But there were islands in the West Indies owned by France, by Spain and by Holland. All of them were good markets for Connecticut goods, and Connecticut men needed markets. Gradually, Connecticut captains began to go even farther asea, following the lead of Massachusetts captains who were developing a triangular trade route which led from their home port to Africa, to the West Indies, then home

again. In Africa, these Puritans from Connecticut found
that they could trade rum and iron bars for African men
and women who had been captured to be sold as slaves.
With no thought for anything but profit, they took the
captured Africans to the islands and sold them there for
sugar, molasses and Spanish dollars. Back home again, they
distilled rum from the molasses and set forth on the cycle
again. Many of the trading ships setting out from New
England were breaking the home country's laws regulating
commerce. They told themselves that the laws were unfair,
and indeed New England men did need markets that
England would not allow them. So they took the markets
they wanted. Some men became smugglers, and some were
slavers, and many grew rich.

Connecticut people were also moving overland across
the country during these years. The colony's territory ran
westward as far as the Pacific Ocean, according to the
charter of 1662. Land granted to William Penn cut across
some of this claim, but Connecticut men felt that their
grant was an earlier one than Penn's and more valid. In
1757 they started a settlement in a particularly beautiful
region north of the Delaware Water Gap that was known as
Wyoming Valley. They had hardly built shelters before
Pennsylvania men who had paid no attention to the region
came on the scene to run them out. Indians attacked them
also. There were skirmishes, massacres and legal battles,
too, as Connecticut fought for this district. Connecticut
set up its government in the area. Representatives from
there went to the Connecticut legislature. Only after the
Revolution did Connecticut finally decide that the difficulties in maintaining the western settlement were too
great. The Wyoming territory became part of Pennsylvania.
Connecticut did manage to retain one vast tract of land
even farther west which was sometimes known as New

Connecticut and sometimes as the Western Reserve. A group of Connecticut men led by Samuel Cleaveland later started a settlement there and planted a slip of Hartford's Charter Oak as a reminder of home. The settlement finally became the great city of Cleveland, Ohio, but that was long after Connecticut had sold that land and put the purchase money into a perpetual fund for the support of schools.

Still another New Connecticut was being founded in the wild mountain areas north of Massachusetts and east of New York, a territory known then as the Hampshire Grants which later became Vermont. Connecticut soldiers, returning home after fighting the French in Montreal, had traveled through this region and thought it would be good land to settle on. They were young men, and once home, they talked to their sweethearts and wives about the land. Many young couples packed up and pioneered in that northern area, buying their land from the colony of New Hampshire to the east. They took with them, as a matter of course, their Connecticut sense of independence and the Connecticut town system.

Two young Connecticut men, Ethan and Ira Allen, were among those who migrated to Vermont. They took a leading part in the struggle that the men of New Connecticut soon had with the great New York landowners to the west who claimed the land which the new settlers had bought from New Hampshire was theirs.

A group of tough fighting men who became known as the Green Mountain Boys rallied around Ethan and Ira Allen. These Green Mountain Boys, many of them born in Connecticut, finally won Vermont's freedom from New York's claims. The skill in wilderness scouting and fighting which they gained in this border warfare was wonderfully helpful to the cause of all the colonies when they united in the Revolution.

Farmers and ship captains, businessmen, peddlers and smugglers, pioneers and inventors and poets—these were the Connecticut Yankees of the middle of the eighteenth century. But by this time they were also something more. Through all the long struggles with the French and the Indians, these Yankees had fought alongside Cavaliers from Virginia and Maryland, burgers from New York, Quakers from Pennsylvania and New Jersey; some had even met the mountain men from the Carolinas and rice and tobacco planters from the far south. Different as they all were, they had begun to sense dimly that they had something more in common with each other than they had with the English regular soldiers who came from overseas to fight with them. They had more in common with each other than they had with any visiting official or royal governor from England. They understood the difficulties the Indians presented, the difficulties of finding markets for their products, the difficulties of the wilderness, in ways that no Englishman straight from England ever could.

It was just then, as the men and women in thirteen colonies were first beginning to feel that they were all Americans, that the English Parliament enacted the Stamp Act, imposing taxes on all the English colonies in America without the colonists having a word to say about them.

XIII. "A General Council Chosen by All..."

The Stamp Act seemed a perfectly reasonable tax to the men of the English Parliament. To them it was simply a method of getting the English colonies in America to contribute a little money to help pay for the soldiers, the ships and the ammunition that were sent periodically to their defense.

To America, where the colonies had been spending men and money for their own defense ever since they had made their first settlements in the new country, the tax was an insult and an outrage that set off a tumult in every one of the thirteen colonies.

Connecticut, committed to no taxation without representation since The Fundamental Orders of 1639, was the first of the colonies to send an agent to London protesting the Stamp Act. Even while the agent was in England, getting nowhere with his arguments, groups who called themselves Sons of Liberty were forming in Connecticut,

Colonists reading the Stamp Act.

as in Massachusetts and other colonies, to rouse everybody to resist the new taxation. Jonathan Trumbull, later to be war governor of Connecticut and one of George Washington's most trusted friends and allies, was heading a popular movement to fight the tax.

Massachusetts sent out a call to all the colonies to meet in a congress to discuss means of resisting the tax. Connecticut quickly sent delegates to New York where the congress was meeting. The delegates from the various colonies were agreed in the need for boycotting English products as well as the hated new tax.

Connecticut's agent to London came home, convinced that the Stamp Act could not be overthrown. Hoping to make its operation easier on his neighbors, he had agreed to be in charge of the tax collections in Connecticut. He was met by a mob when he left his ship at New Haven, and a thousand farmers and freeholders rode behind him all the way to Hartford, shouting insults and demanding that he resign his office. Connecticut men would not pay the stamp tax.

In all the colonies, men were speaking out. Patrick Henry was rousing his compatriots in Virginia, James Otis in Massachusetts. The storm in America grew so great that Parliament was forced to repeal the Stamp Act the very next year. But it was still determined to wring money from the colonies somehow and to put a stop to the illegal free trading that was going on so widely—and so prosperously. New taxes and import duties were imposed as well as new navigation acts that restricted shipping in New England and elsewhere.

The worst troubles of the next years centered in Massachusetts, which had been fretting against its royal governors for years. Connecticut was not the only colony waiting breathlessly for news from there, but Connecticut was the closest and so most ready to rush to its aid. In 1770 British soldiers were stationed in Boston to protect tax collectors from England. They allowed themselves to be provoked into shooting into a crowd. Five Boston men were killed. The first to fall was Crispus Attucks, an Afro-American who had escaped from slavery to make a good life for himself as an American seaman.

This shooting, instantly labeled the Boston Massacre throughout the colonies, provoked new outrage everywhere. Town meetings were held all over Connecticut to appoint committees of safety, to appropriate money for arms and powder and to send whatever aid was needed to Boston.

The next three years were full of tension and argument. Not all colonists sided with the hot-blooded Sons of Liberty. There were those who felt that Parliament and King George had arguments on their side and that their neighbors were heading for disaster with their protests.

Those three years also saw the leaders of the thirteen colonies growing closer than they had ever been before. Committees of Correspondence arranged for letters to go from colony to colony, explaining local grievances and describing how the situation was being met in various areas.

Then, in 1774, Parliament passed a new series of taxes, duties and shipping restrictions applying to the American colonies. The colonists were so horrified by them that they called them the Intolerable Acts.

In Boston, a group of men dumped the cargo of three tea ships into Boston Harbor, and thirteen colonies applauded the Boston Tea Party.

Virginia was the colony that sent out the first call for a meeting of delegates from every colony, to discuss how to further resist the Intolerable Acts. Every colony except Georgia accepted the invitation, and the First Continental Congress met in Philadelphia.

Agitated as all the delegates were, few of them were thinking yet of breaking the colonies' ties with England. Their one concern was how to force Parliament to give up or at least modify its policies toward the colonies.

But Parliament paid no heed to the letters and petitions it received from the First Continental Congress. And the next spring there were clashes between English regular soldiers and the colonial militia at both Lexington and Concord in Massachusetts.

After that, it was as though everything began happening at once. The Second Continental Congress was in session almost before the smoke from the musket fire had cleared. The Connecticut delegates were in their seats along with delegates from all the other colonies. And the first order of business was the creation of a continental army to protect the colonists and their rights.

On the very day that this second Congress was meeting, Ethan Allen and his Green Mountain Boys were marching down from the hills of the "New Connecticut" territory of Vermont toward the English-held Fort Ticonderoga. They stole up on the fort after dark when all was quiet within. Allen hammered on the barred door with his gun butt.

Colonel Israel Putnam.

"Open," he cried, "in the name of the great Jehovah and the Continental Congress."

The door was opened. A startled English officer saw the troops outside and surrendered the fort.

News of the Lexington and Concord fights reached Colonel Israel Putnam in Pomfret, Connecticut, when he was out in his fields plowing. He heard what the messenger had to say, dropped the plow handles, left his oxen harnessed and ran for his fastest horse. Then he galloped to the residence of Governor Jonathan Trumbull for orders. Trumbull told Putnam to proceed to Boston at once. Putnam spent the rest of the afternoon gathering men and horses. Then he mounted his horse again and rode through the night and the next day, covering the hundred and twenty miles to Boston in eighteen hours.

Six regiments of Connecticut troops soon were following him. Among them was young Nathan Hale, a schoolmaster who would later die a brave death and regret that he had but one life to lose for his country. These Connecticut troops joined troops from other colonies who had hastened to Boston and helped in throwing up fortifications near a mound known as Bunker Hill.

Putnam, now a brigadier-general, was in command of the colonial troops when the English regulars attacked these fortifications on June 17. There were twelve hundred colonists facing three thousand advancing English.

"Men, you are all marksmen," Putnam called out. "Don't one of you fire until you see the whites of their eyes."

In the end, the colonists had to retreat before the advancing waves of disciplined regulars, but they had won a victory of sorts all the same. The English had lost over one thousand men to four hundred of the colonists, and they had a new respect for the way the colonists could fight. White Americans and black ones, too, had taken part in the battle, and all had behaved with unflinching courage.

By this time, the Continental Congress had formally voted for a Continental Army and had appointed George Washington to be its commander in chief. A few days after the battle of Bunker Hill, Washington took command of that army which now consisted of fifteen thousand men, three thousand from Connecticut.

The next months were troubled. Those colonists who had never been in favor of defying England were now doing what they could to help the English forces in America and hinder the rebelling colonists. New York was a town with a large number of these loyalists living in it. While Ethan Allen and his men dragged cannon from Fort Ticonderoga over the mountains to George Washington, who was organizing the army outside Boston, Connecticut's General Lee marched down on New York along with

Jonathan Trumbull with his wife and oldest daughter.

twelve hundred Connecticut men. Lee took possession of that doubtful town to hold it until Washington could bring his army from Boston. Later, the redoubtable Israel Putnam was put in command of the city and drove off a British fleet that tried to take it.

The need for more men, more supplies and more money worried Washington endlessly. One man to whom he could always turn was Governor Trumbull of Connecticut, the one colonial governor who was wholeheartedly for the American cause. All the other colonies had royal governors, appointed by the king. Only Connecticut, with its democratic charter, faced the outbreak of war with one of its own men in power. Trumbull was a constant source of help and strength to Washington who called him "Brother Jonathan." (It was a name people would later use as a nickname for the new United States.) Under Trumbull's guidance, Connecticut bore a larger burden of the war expense than any other colony for many months. Washington wrote Trumbull that he needed more help from the

Connecticut assembly. "I am confident they will not be wanting in their exertions for supporting the just and constitutional rights of the colonies." And he was right. Connecticut did not fail him.

When the Third Continental Congress met in Philadelphia in the early summer of 1776, the last and greatest decision had to be made. Were the colonies fighting to free themselves completely from English rule or were they not? Some delegates had come to the congress instructed to vote for independence. Others were unsure. The Connecticut delegates, born and raised in the climate of independence, had no doubts. At last all were agreed. Thomas Jefferson of Virginia was appointed to write the first draft of the Declaration of Independence.

By June of 1776, the delegates from the thirteen colonies were listening to that document being read aloud. They were arguing and debating it, phrase by phrase. When the debate was finally over and the corrections that the delegates wanted had been made, the final draft was adopted by a general vote on July 4. "We hold these truths to be self-evident, that all men are created equal. . . ."

The finished document was not ready for the signatures of the delegates until August 2. Connecticut's four delegates to the Continental Congress had been waiting eagerly. Roger Sherman, the mayor of New Haven, who had helped to write the final draft, signed his name to the Declaration. William Williams of Lebanon, a veteran of the French and Indian War, added his signature. Oliver Wolcott of Litchfield, a veteran of King George's War, a graduate of

Four Connecticut delegates signed the Declaration of Independence: Roger Sherman, Samuel Huntington, William Williams, and Oliver Wolcott. Their signatures can be seen in the last column.

In CONGRESS, July 4, 1776.

The unanimous Declaration of the thirteen united States of America.

When in the Course of human events, it becomes necessary for one people to dissolve the political bands which have connected them with another, and to assume among the powers of the earth, the separate and equal station to which the Laws of Nature and of Nature's God entitle them, a decent respect to the opinions of mankind requires that they should declare the causes which impel them to the separation.

We hold these truths to be self-evident, that all men are created equal, that they are endowed by their Creator with certain unalienable Rights, that among these are Life, Liberty and the pursuit of Happiness.—That to secure these rights, Governments are instituted among Men, deriving their just powers from the consent of the governed,—That whenever any Form of Government becomes destructive of these ends, it is the Right of the People to alter or to abolish it, and to institute new Government, laying its foundation on such principles and organizing its powers in such form, as to them shall seem most likely to effect their Safety and Happiness. Prudence, indeed, will dictate that Governments long established should not be changed for light and transient causes; and accordingly all experience hath shewn, that mankind are more disposed to suffer, while evils are sufferable, than to right themselves by abolishing the forms to which they are accustomed. But when a long train of abuses and usurpations, pursuing invariably the same Object evinces a design to reduce them under absolute Despotism, it is their right, it is their duty, to throw off such Government, and to provide new Guards for their future security.—Such has been the patient sufferance of these Colonies; and such is now the necessity which constrains them to alter their former Systems of Government. The history of the present King of Great Britain is a history of repeated injuries and usurpations, all having in direct object the establishment of an absolute Tyranny over these States. To prove this, let Facts be submitted to a candid world.

He has refused his Assent to Laws, the most wholesome and necessary for the public good.

He has forbidden his Governors to pass Laws of immediate and pressing importance, unless suspended in their operation till his Assent should be obtained; and when so suspended, he has utterly neglected to attend to them.

He has refused to pass other Laws for the accommodation of large districts of people, unless those people would relinquish the right of Representation in the Legislature, a right inestimable to them and formidable to tyrants only.

He has called together legislative bodies at places unusual, uncomfortable, and distant from the depository of their public Records, for the sole purpose of fatiguing them into compliance with his measures.

He has dissolved Representative Houses repeatedly, for opposing with manly firmness his invasions on the rights of the people.

He has refused for a long time, after such dissolutions, to cause others to be elected; whereby the Legislative powers, incapable of Annihilation, have returned to the People at large for their exercise; the State remaining in the mean time exposed to all the dangers of invasion from without, and convulsions within.

He has endeavoured to prevent the population of these States; for that purpose obstructing the Laws for Naturalization of Foreigners; refusing to pass others to encourage their migrations hither, and raising the conditions of new Appropriations of Lands.

He has obstructed the Administration of Justice, by refusing his Assent to Laws for establishing Judiciary powers.

He has made Judges dependent on his Will alone, for the tenure of their offices, and the amount and payment of their salaries.

He has erected a multitude of New Offices, and sent hither swarms of Officers to harrass our people, and eat out their substance.

He has kept among us, in times of peace, Standing Armies without the Consent of our legislatures.

He has affected to render the Military independent of and superior to the Civil power.

He has combined with others to subject us to a jurisdiction foreign to our constitution, and unacknowledged by our laws; giving his Assent to their Acts of pretended Legislation:

For quartering large bodies of armed troops among us:

For protecting them, by a mock Trial, from punishment for any Murders which they should commit on the Inhabitants of these States:

For cutting off our Trade with all parts of the world:

For imposing Taxes on us without our Consent:

For depriving us in many cases, of the benefits of Trial by Jury:

For transporting us beyond Seas to be tried for pretended offences:

For abolishing the free System of English Laws in a neighbouring Province, establishing therein an Arbitrary government, and enlarging its Boundaries so as to render it at once an example and fit instrument for introducing the same absolute rule into these Colonies:

For taking away our Charters, abolishing our most valuable Laws, and altering fundamentally the Forms of our Governments:

For suspending our own Legislatures, and declaring themselves invested with power to legislate for us in all cases whatsoever.

He has abdicated Government here, by declaring us out of his Protection and waging War against us.

He has plundered our seas, ravaged our Coasts, burnt our towns, and destroyed the lives of our people.

He is at this time transporting large Armies of foreign Mercenaries to compleat the works of death, desolation and tyranny, already begun with circumstances of Cruelty & perfidy scarcely paralleled in the most barbarous ages, and totally unworthy the Head of a civilized nation.

He has constrained our fellow Citizens taken Captive on the high Seas to bear Arms against their Country, to become the executioners of their friends and Brethren, or to fall themselves by their Hands.

He has excited domestic insurrections amongst us, and has endeavoured to bring on the inhabitants of our frontiers, the merciless Indian Savages, whose known rule of warfare, is an undistinguished destruction of all ages, sexes and conditions.

In every stage of these Oppressions We have Petitioned for Redress in the most humble terms: Our repeated Petitions have been answered only by repeated injury. A Prince, whose character is thus marked by every act which may define a Tyrant, is unfit to be the ruler of a free people.

Nor have We been wanting in attentions to our British brethren. We have warned them from time to time of attempts by their legislature to extend an unwarrantable jurisdiction over us. We have reminded them of the circumstances of our emigration and settlement here. We have appealed to their native justice and magnanimity, and we have conjured them by the ties of our common kindred to disavow these usurpations, which, would inevitably interrupt our connections and correspondence. They too have been deaf to the voice of justice and of consanguinity. We must, therefore, acquiesce in the necessity, which denounces our Separation, and hold them, as we hold the rest of mankind, Enemies in War, in Peace Friends.

We, therefore, the Representatives of the united States of America, in General Congress, Assembled, appealing to the Supreme Judge of the world for the rectitude of our intentions, do, in the Name, and by Authority of the good People of these Colonies, solemnly publish and declare, That these United Colonies are, and of Right ought to be Free and Independent States; that they are Absolved from all Allegiance to the British Crown, and that all political connection between them and the State of Great Britain, is and ought to be totally dissolved; and that as Free and Independent States, they have full Power to levy War, conclude Peace, contract Alliances, establish Commerce, and to do all other Acts and Things which Independent States may of right do. And for the support of this Declaration, with a firm reliance on the protection of divine Providence, we mutually pledge to each other our Lives, our Fortunes and our sacred Honor.

John Hancock

Button Gwinnett
Lyman Hall
Geo Walton

Wm Hooper
Joseph Hewes
John Penn

Edward Rutledge
Thos Heyward Junr.
Thomas Lynch Junr.
Arthur Middleton

Samuel Chase
Wm Paca
Thos Stone
Charles Carroll of Carrollton
George Wythe
Richard Henry Lee
Th Jefferson
Benja Harrison
Thos Nelson jr.
Francis Lightfoot Lee
Carter Braxton

Robt Morris
Benjamin Rush
Benja Franklin
John Morton
Geo Clymer
Jas Smith
Geo Taylor
James Wilson
Geo. Ross
Caesar Rodney
Geo Read
Tho M:Kean

Wm Floyd
Phil. Livingston
Frans Lewis
Lewis Morris
Richd Stockton
Jno Witherspoon
Fras Hopkinson
John Hart
Abra Clark

Josiah Bartlett
Wm Whipple
Saml Adams
John Adams
Robt Treat Paine
Elbridge Gerry
Step Hopkins
William Ellery
Roger Sherman
Sam'el Huntington
Wm Williams
Oliver Wolcott
Matthew Thornton

Yale and a commissioner to the Iroquois Indians after the Albany Congress, was another signer for Connecticut. Finally there was Samuel Huntington of Windham. In the next years he became president of the Continental Congress and later, a governor of Connecticut after the war.

As one Connecticut man after another wrote his name on the parchment, Connecticut tradition since the writing of The Fundamental Orders in Hartford, in 1639, was helping to guide their pens.

The story was not over. The story was just beginning as Connecticut, proud and independent for so long, joined twelve other American colonies who were going to fight for their mutual independence together. The words of Thomas Hooker could have spoken for them all. "In matters of greater consequence, which concern the common good, a general council, chosen by all, I conceive, under favor, most suitable to rule and most safe for the relief of all."

BIBLIOGRAPHY

BALDWIN, ERNEST H., *Stories of Old New Haven*. New York: The Abbey Press, 1902.

BLACK, ROBERT C., III, *The Younger John Winthrop*. New York: Columbia University Press, 1966.

DWIGHT, THEODORE, JR., *The History of Connecticut*. New York: Harper & Bros., 1842.

EARLE, ALICE MORSE, *Home Life in Colonial Days*. New York: Macmillan, 1926.

GOCHER, W. H., *Wadsworth, or the Charter Oak*. Hartford, Conn.: W.H. Gocher, 1904.

HART, ALBERT BUSHNELL, *Colonial Children*. New York: Macmillan, 1930.

HOLLISTER, GIDEON HIRAM, *The History of Connecticut*. Hartford: Case, Tiffany & Co., 1857.

JOHNSTON, ALEXANDER, *Connecticut, a Study of Commonwealth-Democracy*. Boston & New York: Houghton, Mifflin & Co., 1903.

MILLS, LEWIS SPRAGUE, M. A., *The Story of Connecticut*. West Rindge, N.H.: Richard R. Smith Publisher, Inc., 1958.

PRESCOTT, DELLA R., *A Day in a Colonial Home*. Francestown, N.H.: Marshall Jones Co., 1921.

SHEPARD, ODELL. *Connecticut, Past and Present*. New York: Alfred Knopf, 1939.

TODD, CHARLES BURR, *In Olde Connecticut*. New York: The Grafton Press, 1906.

WOODWARD, WILLIAM E., *The Way Our People Lived*. New York: Liveright Publishing Co., 1963.

IMPORTANT DATES

1614—Dutch Captain Adrian Block sails along Connecticut coast, explores Connecticut River.

1631—River Indian chief, Waginacut, visits governors of Massachusetts Bay and Plymouth colonies, inviting English settlers to Connecticut territory.

1632—Governor Edward Winslow of Plymouth makes expedition to Connecticut River; buys land.

—Dutch plan a fort at mouth of Connecticut River.

1633—Dutch send Jacob Van Curler to build a fort up the river, near present site of Hartford.

—Plymouth colony sends William Holmes to build an English fort a few miles up the river from the Dutch fort. Dutch try to drive the English away but instead retreat themselves.

—The Reverend Thomas Hooker and his congregation land in Boston.

1634—John Oldham, of Watertown, Massachusetts, leads group of Massachusetts colonists into Connecticut and founds town of Wethersfield.

1635—More Massachusetts people emigrate to Connecticut and found town of Windsor, not far from Wethersfield.

—(Autumn) Fort Saybrook established by John Winthrop, Jr., at mouth of Connecticut River.

1636—A small Massachusetts group settles upriver near Wethersfield and Windsor, founding third river town of Hartford.

—(April) David Gardiner born at Fort Saybrook—first white child born in Connecticut.

—Thomas Hooker and his congregation walk through wilderness from Massachusetts to join settlers at Hartford.

—John Oldham, founder of Wethersfield, killed by Pequot Indians.

1636–37—Pequot attacks on Fort Saybrook, then on Wethersfield.

1637—(May) Connecticut colonists declare war on Pequots.

—(Summer) Pequot fort destroyed and Indians massacred. Pequot power broken forever.

—The Reverend John Davenport, Theophilus Eaton and two hundred of Davenport's congregation arrive in Boston from England.

1638—(March) The Davenport-Eaton group emigrate to Connecticut and settle at mouth of Quinnipiac River, founding New Haven Colony.

—(May 31) Hooker's sermon on democracy.

1639—(January) Connecticut's Fundamental Orders adopted—first written constitution in history.

1639—New Haven Colony buys more land and founds towns of Milford, Guilford, and Stamford, also Southold on Long Island.

—New Haven's church-controlled government established.

—George Fenwick becomes governor of Saybrook.

1640—New Haven colonists start a settlement on Delaware River but are driven away by Dutch and Swedes.

1641—First Free School established in New Haven Colony.

1642—First legally established school in Hartford.

1643—A New England Union formed by Massachusetts, Plymouth, Connecticut, New Haven and Saybrook colonies, for mutual protection against the Dutch and the Indians.

1644—Connecticut Colony buys the Saybrook Colony and its royal grant from George Fenwick.

1647—New Haven Colony sends off "Great Shippe" to England.

1648—The phantom ship appears in New Haven harbor.

1650—New Amsterdam governor Peter Stuyvesant presses Dutch claims in Connecticut but is generally unsuccessful.

1654—English seize Dutch fort near Hartford, and Dutch lose last holding in Connecticut.

1660—Puritan Commonwealth in England ends; Charles II on the throne. Regicide judges take refuge in New Haven Colony and are sheltered there for four years.

1662—John Winthrop, Jr., governor of the Connecticut Colony, goes to England and obtains charter for the colony from Charles II, winning virtual independence for the colony.

1664—Charles II grants Connecticut and New Netherlands territory to his brother, James, Duke of York and Albany. English fleet takes New Amsterdam.

1665—New Haven Colony merges with Connecticut Colony.

1670—Alarms in Massachusetts about Indian chief, King Philip.

1673—Sir Edmund Andros appointed by James, Duke of York, as governor of Connecticut and New York territories.

1675—Connecticut militia fight in King Philip's War in Massachusetts.

—Andros tries to take control of Connecticut but does not succeed.

1682—Andros recalled to England.

1685—Charles II dead; James II, new king of England, plans central government for New England. Andros appointed governor.

1687—(October 31) Andros arrives in Hartford to demand charter. Charter hidden in oak tree. Andros takes over government of colony.

1689—Andros out of power. Connecticut again functions under original charter.

1689–97—King William's War—against French and Indians. Unsuccessful attempt to take Quebec from French.

1701—First beginnings of a college in Connecticut.

1702–13—Queen Anne's war—again against the French allied with the Indians. Another unsuccessful attempt to take Quebec, but Nova Scotia is won from France.

1717—Yale College established in New Haven and first building erected.

1739–42—War of Jenkins Ear—an English quarrel with Spain. Connecticut men join in an expedition to South America.

1744–48—King George's War. The French fortress Louisburg, on Cape Breton, captured by colonists and English regulars. Fortress later ceded back to France by England.

1754—Seven New England colonies send delegates to Albany, New York, for a congress to plan mutual defense against French and Indians.

1757—Connecticut people start a western settlement in Wyoming Valley near Delaware Water Gap.

1758–60—French and Indian War. Connecticut men help retake Louisburg fortress, also Fort Ticonderoga. Colonel Israel Putnam fights alongside General Wolfe in a successful attempt to capture Quebec. French power in America broken.

1764—*The Hartford Courant* established, the longest continuously published newspaper in America.

1765—The Stamp Act passed by Parliament. An agent sent from Connecticut to London to protest. Sons of Liberty organized. Connecticut delegates attend a congress of all the colonies in New York.

1770—Ethan and Ira Allen and other Connecticut people begin settling in the New Hampshire Grants, the "New Connecticut" that later became Vermont.

—Boston Massacre in Massachusetts. Connecticut appointing committees of safety and sending aid to Massachusetts.

1774—The Intolerable Acts passed by Parliament. Tea dumped in the harbor in Boston. First Continental Congress called and held in Philadelphia.

1775—Skirmishes between English soldiers and colonists at Lexington and Concord. Second Continental Congress in session. Ethan Allen and Green Mountain Boys take Fort Ticonderoga from the English. Israel Putnam commands colonial forces at Bunker Hill. Governor Jonathan Trumbull helps General Washington with men, money and supplies.

1776—The Declaration of Independence drafted, debated on, finally signed by delegates from all thirteen colonies—four delegates from Connecticut.

PLACES TO VISIT

Among the many historic sites in Connecticut which readers of this book will find of interest are:

FARMINGTON

FARMINGTON MUSEUM (STANLEY-WHITMAN HOUSE CA. 1660). 37 High Street. A fine seventeenth-century house. 10 A.M.–NOON, 2–5 P.M.: April-November, Tuesday-Saturday, December-March, Friday-Saturday; Sunday all year from 2 P.M.; closed Thanksgiving, December 25. Admission 50¢; under 12, free.

GREENWICH

PUTNAM COTTAGE. 243 East Putnam Avenue. General Israel Putnam escaped from the British in 1779 from this house, which is now maintained as a museum by the D.A.R. Open Monday, Thursday-Saturday, 10 A.M.–5 P.M.; closed January 1, Thanksgiving, and December 25. Admission 50¢; children, free.

GUILFORD

HENRY WHITFIELD HOUSE (1639). State Historical Museum. Two and a half miles south on Whitfield Street, this building has been restored with seventeenth-century furnishings including a herb garden. There are also craft exhibits. This is possibly the oldest stone house in this area. Daily except Monday and holidays: April-October, 10 A.M–5 P.M.; November-December 14, January 16-March to 4 P.M.; closed December 15–January 15. Admission 50¢.

HARTFORD

CONNECTICUT HISTORICAL SOCIETY. 1 Elizabeth Street. Contains a library and museum and has one of the two copies of the Connecticut Charter of Charles II. Daily except Sunday and holidays. Museum: 1–5 P.M.; library: 9:30 A.M.–5:30 P.M. June-August, Saturdays to noon. Free.

WADSWORTH ATHENEUM. 590 Main Street. This is one of the country's major art museums with costumes, armor, porcelains, Pilgrim furniture, and other collections in four buildings. Open Tuesday-Saturday, 10 A.M.–5 P.M., Sunday, 1–6 P.M. Closed January 1, July 4, Thanksgiving, and December 25. Free.

CONNECTICUT STATE LIBRARY. 231 Capitol Avenue. Law, social science, history, genealogy collections and official state archives are prominent in this library. Also exhibited are the Colt Collection of Firearms; Connecticut memorabilia, including original colonial charter and Indian artifacts. Open Monday-Friday, 8:30 A.M.–5 P.M., Saturday, 9 A.M.–1 P.M., closed Sunday and holidays. Freee.

CHARTER OAK TREE MONUMENT. Charter Oak Avenue.

NEW HAVEN

PARDEE-MORRIS HOUSE. 325 Lighthouse Road. This house was built in 1685 and burned in 1779 by the British. It was rebuilt in 1780 using the masonry that was left. It has American primitive and period furnishings, an herb garden, coaches and coach house. May-October, Monday-Friday, 10 A.M.–5 P.M.; Sunday from 2 P.M.; closed Saturday, holidays and November-April. Contribution.

YALE UNIVERSITY (1701). In center of town. The old campus is particularly worth seeing. Nathan Hale once roomed at Connecticut Hall. Tours leave Visitor Center, College Street, summer, daily, 10:30 A.M., 1:30 P.M., 3 P.M. Free.

WEST ROCK PARK. Wintergreen Avenue, one and a half miles northwest of Judges Cave. This was used as a hiding place for two regicides in 1661. The nature center has small animals that are native to the state as well as butterflies and other insects. Picnic area. Daily sunrise-sunset. Free.

NEW LONDON

NATHAN HALE SCHOOLHOUSE. School where Hale once taught. June-September 15, Tuesday-Sunday, 1–4 P.M. Closed rest of the year. Free.

NORWICH

TANTAQUIDGEON INDIAN MUSEUM. 1819 Norwich-New London Road. Five miles south on Connecticut 32 in Uncasville. The museum contains works of New England Indian tribes. May-October, daily, 10 A.M.–6 P.M. Closed rest of the year. Donation.

Times and admission prices are subject to change without notice.

INDEX

Terry, Eli, 112
Thomas, Seth, 112
Treat, Robert, 90–91, 95–96
Trumbull, Jonathan, 118, 121, 123–24

Uncas, 21, 22, 24, 25, 26, 29, 31

Van Curler, Jacob, 6, 7, 8
Vane, Sir Henry, 23
Van Twiller, Wouter, 6, 9
Virginia Colony, 5, 22, 106, 119, 124

Wadsworth, Joseph, 96
Waginacut, 1–2, 3, 4, 5, 6, 19
War of Jenkins' Ear, 105
Warwick, Earl of, 15
Warwick, Grant, 67
Warwick Patent, 63, 81
Washington, George, 106, 107, 108, 118, 122, 123–24
Washington, Lawrence, 106
Webster, Noah, 112–13

Whaling industry, 49
Whalley, Edward, 75–77
Whitney, Eli, 112
William of Orange, 94, 98
Williams, Roger, 18, 24
Williams, William, 124
Winslow, Edward, 2, 6, 7, 8, 9
Winthrop, Fitz John, 98, 105
Winthrop, Governor John, 2, 7, 12, 73, 14, 15, 22
Winthrop, Jr., John, 15, 16, 17, 59, 78–80, 81, 82, 88, 95
Witchcraft, 100–01
Wolcott, Jr., Henry, 33
Wolcott, Oliver, 124
Wolfe, General, 108
Wopigwooitt, 21, 22
Wyllys, Samuel, 83, 90

Yale, Elihu, 102–03
Yale College, 101–03, 124
"Yankee peddlers," 111
York, Duke of, *see* James II